Grace-Filled Transitions Unto Transformation:

Adapting the 12 Steps for a New Vision of Spiritual Eldering

By Angelita Fenker D.Min.

Grace-Filled Transitions Unto Transformation:

Adapting the 12 Steps for a
New Vision of Spiritual Eldering

by Angelita Fenker, D.Min.

The Rhodes-Fulbright Library

Copyright ©2004 by Angelita Fenker

All Rights Reserved

Cover Photo: Angelita Fenker (The apple tree symbolizes family: Past-Present-Future)

ISBN: 1-55605-371-1

Library of Congress Control Number: **2004113688**

WYNDHAM HALL PRESS
Lima, Ohio 45806
www.wyndhamhallpress.com

Printed in The United States of America

Grace-Filled Transitions Unto Transformation:

Adapting the 12 Steps for a New Vision of Spiritual Eldering

****

A Tribute to a Christ-centered, Eldering Person of Faith

Blessed are you, Eldering Person of Faith!
You are standing tall, yet rooted deep in your lived wisdom,
In the awareness of your eternal belovedness.

You are touching the world with your tremendous love.
You are transforming the heart of the universe
Through the dynamic Christ-centered love
That flows through you and mentors
everyone your life touches.

This very power ennobles your entire life
And enables others to feel good
about themselves in your presence.
Blessed are you as your soul magnifies the Lord
And rejoices in God your Savior,
For he who is mighty truly has done wonderful things
To, with, in and through you, because of your love,
To change the world around you!

Rejoice! Be glad! Christ's life in you is full!
The Incarnation continues--in YOU!
Truly! Blessed are you, Eldering Person of Faith!
Walk tall, and let your whole being sing "Yes" forever!

--Angelita Fenker

Dedication

I dedicate this book to my loving parents,
Frank L. (1901-1985) and Mary E. (Alberding) Fenker (1899-1999),
of whom I have always been very proud.
They are forever held in God's heart, and mine.

The Format and Focus of this Book

*This material was originally created for retreats with groups of recovering Ministers who wanted something on 'aging.' Its Christ-centered focus stresses wellness and empowerment. It is useful for personal enrichment, and as a facilitator's handbook for group use. The book is for anyone, whether officially in 'recovery' or not, since every adult is recovering from something which needs healing. Writing in the book is strongly recommended so that it becomes a tool to **use** on the journey toward becoming a spiritual-elder-sage, and not just something to be lightly read, and then forgotten.*

The outline-format serves a distinct purpose: it presents material in a brief, easy-to-read manner, and allows for personal notes to be penned-in so that it becomes a reflection-workbook. This is especially helpful when used with a group. The book becomes user-involved, and helps to maintain a growth-focus for one's journey.

The underlying theme of this book is that as long as we choose to give and receive love, we'll never get old. We can't help 'growing older,' but each of us must decide whether our emphasis is on 'growing,' or 'older,' Read it and decide for yourself.

Permission from Alcoholics Anonymous World Services, Inc.

The Twelve Steps are adapted and a brief excerpt from the book, *Alcoholics Anonymous* is reprinted with permission of Alcoholics Anonymous World Services, Inc. (AAWS) Permission to adapt the Twelve Steps and reprint a brief excerpt from the book, *Alcoholics Anonymous* does not mean that A.A.W.S. has reviewed or approved the contents of this publication, or that A.A.W.S. necessarily agrees with the views expressed herein. *A.A.* is a program of recovery from alcoholism only -use of the Twelve Steps in connection with programs and activities which are patterned after A.A., but which address other problems, or in any other non-A.A. context, does not imply otherwise.

THE TWELVE STEPS OF ALCOHOLICS ANONYMOUS

1. We admitted we were powerless over alcohol--that our lives had become unmanageable. .

2. Came to believe that a Power greater than ourselves could restore us to sanity.

3. Made a decision to turn our will and our lives over to the care of God as we understood Him.

4. Made a searching and fearless moral inventory of ourselves.

5. Admitted to God, to ourselves, and to another human being the exact nature of our wrongs.

6. Were entirely ready to have God remove all these defects of character.

7. Humbly asked Him to remove our shortcomings.

8. Made a list of all persons we had harmed, and became willing to make amends to them all.

9. Made direct amends to such people wherever possible, except when to do so would injure them or others.

10. Continued to take personal inventory and when we were wrong promptly admitted it.

11. Sought through prayer and meditation to improve our conscious contact with God as we understood Him, praying only for knowledge of His will for us and the power to carry that out.

12. Having had a spiritual awakening as the result of these Steps, we tried to carry this message to alcoholics, and to practice these principles in all our affairs.

Alcoholics Anonymous World Services, Inc. ®

Contents

COMMENTS and INTRODUCTION

A few comments at the start will help us to know where we came from, where we hope to go, and where our vision-quest-commitment can take us at this time in our lives. Centenarians are no longer rare in our society. Scientists who study the physical dimensions of aging have determined that human beings were meant to live a quality life, have healthy years, and a creative mind to at *least* 120 years of age--barring some unforeseen accident or illness. Though biological signs of cellular aging begin between ages 11 and 12 and speed-of-reaction begins to slow at about age 20, (PBS, 2003, *Stealing Time*, Warshofsky), the human brain can continue to develop and mature for as long as we live if it is cared for.

What's more, there is a growing effort on the part of many who study the aging process to join forces in the pursuit of knowledge regarding not only the aging process itself, but also to take an in-depth look at the *way* each discipline approaches this reality. Because of the longevity factor, ours is the first society which can view the present aging population through the entire human life-cycle: mentally, physically, educationally, relationally, psychologically, socially, and above all, spiritually. Especially in this latter category, we can no longer solve the problems of our maturing age with the tools and methods we used in the past, any more than we can use former methods of medical treatment to help with today's cures. It simply will not work. Trying to adhere to a spirituality and a spiritual-methodology which fit our past would be like trying to continue to eat pabulum when we have outgrown babyhood.

As we shift from a mainly youth-oriented culture to one of more mature balance, then each of the disciplines involved in helping us to develop and grow *must* provide new services, new concepts and even new careers in order to help meet the needs, and reasonable wants, of millions of diverse older people. If this does not happen, we will be infantilizing millions; spiritual growth will not take place. The more we age, the more we are *unlike* others in our age group; the younger a person is, the more he/she is like the rest of their peers. Because of this eldering difference, we must be offered more and varied spiritual helps.

Aging is not a disease or a medical condition to be 'cured.' Social and behavioral scientists are now recognizing that vital aspects of adult life have been severely neglected by lack of study for the spiritual and religious concerns of maturing adults--which gives this false, down-hill impression. Churches and religious communities of all denominations have ignored the knowledge about aging which has accumulated in the last fifty years which would have helped them to better serve their maturing adults. According to recent studies, most of a parish's expendable money goes to programs for children and teens; less than one percent goes to help enrich the adults who build and support the parish. As a rule, parish leaders still feed their adult congregations the bare essential nutrition to sustain their spiritual life--nutrition which fit another and less informed generation. St. Paul was even aware of this when he challenged the early Christians to 'become new yeast' in the dough, and to live on more than milk!

What we think and do about our lives as we grow older will have an impact on how our institutions (especially church and society) will have to change in order to meet the needs of maturing adults now and in the future. Open attitudes toward aging must begin with *us*. Each one has to trade in old ideas and knowledge about aging. We have to make sure that religious and secular communities become more cooperative and less argumentative about what we know or do not know regarding eldering. Each of us must throw off the old wine-skins, and the inevitable-slippery-slope-to-deterioration attitude which has become so much a part of our youth-oriented society. We cannot buy into 'agism' any more, even with the 'over the hill' birthday parties so rampant today. We must *rebel*, if that's what is needed, and become the new voice 'in the wilderness.'

The coined word *eldering* used herein has a definite purpose. Any other word which speaks of getting older seems dead-ended: old, senior, aged, etc.. There is no activity happening. When we're runn*ing*, jump*ing*, etc., we're *doing something about our life; the* noun used as a verb indicates action. It urges us toward positive energy in our maturing.

When was the last time we heard about a 'theology of aging' in any official church teaching? We need to change that, and in so-doing, must join other faith communities to learn how they, and cultures much older than the American one, address issues of getting older from a spiritual, theological standpoint. We must produce scholars within the Christian Community with vision, who are not afraid to articulate a new spirituality about eldering. We need men and women who, like Chardin, Rahner and others, will not be afraid to challenge limited views within present church teaching. We need those who will not be timid about sharing knowledge with other religious and social disciplines in order to make creative and innovative strides in this burgeoning area of study and growth. The heart and core of healthy aging is to *become a spiritual-elder-sage*. It needs a theology.

We are not physical beings with a spirit, we are *spiritual beings* with a physical nature on a human journey. We can only experience the Divine through our senses, and can only enable the Divine in those whose lives we touch in the same way. Whatever we do in word or deed, we do all in Christ who strengthens us for mission and ministry. We become a Christ-presence upon the face of the earth by his power in us. Even though he was God, he did not deem this as something to be grasped at. He humbled himself in the likeness of a human being, but it was always his God-Spirit that acted with, through, and in him to change the world around him. *It's the same with us*; no matter how much older we get, our spirit, our life-force within us, *never ages*. If we learn all we can about caring for our body which encloses our spirit, we are always open. In this openness, we'll grow spiritually through our transitions unto transformation--*eternal* transformation--because we will remain vitally connected to our Life Source, Christ.

In an interview at age eighty Karl Rahner, a theologian, said: "*The real highpoint of my life is still to come. I mean the abyss of the mystery of God, into which one lets oneself fall in complete confidence of being caught up by God's love and mercy forever.*" He 'had it together,' so to speak. It's not just that aging brings one face-to-face with one's mortality, for death is only a one time experience. Maturing, however, through aging, takes place over many years, from our birth onward, and comprises a series of transitions and crises that force our attention to ultimate realities. In the process, we change our self-understanding of both life and death, and we grow into a spiritual-elder-sage.

Our society has lost its respect for the wisdom of its older population. It views life as a long, active period, to be followed only by another long time of 'slipping over the hill' into inactivity, declining health, boredom, disability, uselessness, isolation and dependence. We, in church and society, do loving things *for* people who fit this societal norm. However, we do very little to enable, empower, enrich, or tap into the lived wisdom of the older generations, or to call them forth *to do for us*. No one at any age knows what it's like to be that age; nor, until recently, have there been any positive predictions as to what to expect, or what can be done to make the most of the second half of life. This stage has mostly been muddled through. On some behavioral science fronts, this is beginning to change, *slowly*; however, this change has not come to the forefront in society or church. Think of what the world is losing! Older people who have made tremendous contributions to the world over the centuries have done so amid much neglect, criticism, objection, put-downs, and hardship of all sorts. **We** can change this if we will work together--but first, *we must change our own attitude toward 'agism*!'

There is in each of us a Spirit which is able to shake us and take us to where none of us has ever been before. It is possible for us to journey together and to make a real difference if our spirits are open to help and respect one another on our way to becoming a spiritual-elder-sage. At the age in which we are right now, we can share insights, wisdom, and love in order to reclaim, refresh and renew our spiritual powers in Christ-filled dynamic ways, so we can face *transitions unto transformation* at each new time of life. Then, we can also empower and enable others to open up and speak out against agism. We do this through focused awareness, planned action, and Christ's Power in us.

Planning for our oncoming years is vital for success in *living* them. If we are open to the Spirit who is deepening Christ's presence, power, and radiant love within us *now*, we will be able to share the journey, learn from each other, and emerge during our creative transitions unto a transformation in ways we never experienced before. This powerful energy, freshly released, gives us new courage, new hope, new visions, new dreams, and a more vibrant love that we never knew we had inside us. This higher, positive energy gives us a renewed sensitivity to the emergence of an unexamined, untouched, dynamic life still to be generated in us. Our open 'yes' to *this time of life* gives the Spirit free reign.

Socrates said that an unexamined life is not worth living. This is true also is true of us, especially spiritually. Together, we will learn to experience the wisdom of *Sophia* within us. We will then be better able to connect with Christ and one another, and to dwell more on what unites us, rather than on what divides us, on our journey. In this process, we will grow through our transitions unto our own personal, energized transformation. This growth will ready us for the ultimate Peak Transformation we each will experience someday--through, with, and in Christ eternally. As we live in the radiant energy of Christ's power in us, we'll be able to transmit this radiance to everyone and everything that our life touches.

Prayerfully, we enter into this next part of our journey together. As we revisit our own lives with compassion, forgiveness, and openness, we'll be able to form creative visions of where we can yet go. We trust our own insights and deep longings so that we may be more aware of, and attentive to, the sacred within us. The Spirit will help us find the tremendous love we have yet inside of us, so that we may give more of it to the world. Christ said that he came to bring *life* to us...*in abundance* (Jn 10:10). We're called to do the same *now* in our transitions unto transformation. We recall the words of Robert Browning: ***"The best is yet to be, the last of life for which the first was made."***

Let us believe this, and--with Christ's empowerment--act accordingly!

Step 1: Choosing a Positive Attitude

We admitted we were powerless over alcohol--
that our lives had become unmanageable.

We admitted that we are powerless over the eldering process--some things we cannot change, some things we can; what we can change, we will.

Promise 1: We will know a new freedom and a new happiness.

We'll know new freedoms, possibilities, and ways of being in our eldering.

****

I. The most important preparation for our eldering process is *our attitude toward it.* Grace-filled transitions through our maturing effects transformation. These transitions enable and empower us to put on Christ's attitude more fully at each new stage of life.

A. Our potential for transformation in our maturing years is mostly defined by our *attitude* toward the aging process in general--and toward our own in particular. Growth in this time of life is *very important;* our *attitude* gives us *control* over it.

1. Previous transitions have led to this one. In our other stages of maturing we did not have the same control over our life; this one we *do* because we've *lived!*

2. *Attitude* is the first thing we must look at; we can confirm or change it.

3. We remember: "Grow old along with me. The best is yet to be; the last of life for which the first was made." (Robert Browning)

4. Some basic rules to keep in mind are:

a. *Never* treat ourselves as 'old.'
b. *Never* treat an older person as 'old.'
c. *Never* let anyone treat us as 'old.'

B. We see the changes taking place. We can affirm our own humanness, recognize a need for a deeper transformation of attitude (especially in our spirituality), and see a need to verbalize a new way of understanding ourselves and of relating to God, self, others and the world. *Threats of decline can be transformed into spiritual opportunities wherein we enhance our basic self-worth and express new love.*

1. There are losses, but also rebirths and gains. The pain felt is not merely the pain of something dying; it is rather the pain of something new being born. The emphasis is on new life and love; fresh visions and dreams are generated.

    a. All life is a series of losses: we lose the womb to become born; we lose babyhood to become a toddler, etc.. We must lose one phase of life before we can move to the next; all maturing _requires_ change and loss.

    b. Our _attitude_ toward life's losses is the key to spiritual growth. As we choose to focus on _gains_ from loss*es,* and are able to discover our latent potential. We can view our maturing years as a time to develop even more of the wondrous gifts with which God has endowed us. Instead of bemoaning losses of previous years, we focus on the resurrection-gains, and move ahead.

2. Our gain-focus holds many transitions through which we must pass. Each transition can, and must, lead to further transformation, or we'll 'die' inside.

3. A maturing person's greatest tragedy is not in making mistakes on life's journey, but in settling for the status quo, and opting for stagnation. We cannot respond to today's growth-needs with yesterday's tools.

C. In our growth toward transformation, we need to develop a new inwardness, a change of heart and attitude not needed the same way heretofore. We are called to a more contemplative, creative way of being in the world amid our continuing responsibilities. Contemplation leads to fresh ways of viewing and living our life.

1. We deliberately create this _contemplative time of life_ as we consciously choose to deepen our awareness of Christ's presence and action through, with, and in us to change the world around us. We have much love to give yet.

II. If we view our eldering as the richest time of life, we'll not merely drift into our next decade. We'll prepare for it, treasure it, look for ways to enrich it, and live it to the hilt.

A. As we become aware of the tremendous, untapped resources we have yet to find within us, we can look forward to maturing into a vibrant spiritual-elder-sage.

1. We choose to move ahead 'one day at a time,' to be alive, active, energetic, positive, lifelong learners through each new transition unto transformation

B. Becoming a spiritual-elder-sage takes much challenging, personal work, work which is rewarding and fruitful for ourselves, the church, society, and the world.

1. We have the courage to choose life because our spirit is as young as when God first created it. _New life_ awaits us in our next transition-maturing stage.

C. With a positive attitude, enthusiasm, and a loving, cheerful outlook, we trust in God who anoints us into our next maturing transition. We are empowered to grow in wisdom and experience with others through activities which support and determine our successful eldering, so that we'll not die with our dreams unborn.

1. To do this, we must: (a) eat healthily; (b) exercise, even if only waving arms from a bed or chair, (c) socialize; (d) learn something new every day; (e) create 'fun-time' daily; and (f) deepen friendship with Christ through contemplation.

III. We are powerless over getting older, but there are practical things we can do to keep from getting *old.* These help us to expand our spirit and to 'color outside of the lines.'

A. We need to do a life-review (it's best to keep a journal) in order to see how God's loving hand has been upon us every moment to make our lives fruitful.

B. *WE:*

1. Look at our past: create a *keep file* in which we put all the good things we've accomplished, and then create a *wisdom file* into which we place the things we've learned through our mistakes and weaknesses. Both are needed.

2. Recall things we've always wanted to do: plan to do something about those interests we never had, or made, the time to do; we need to be specific.

3. Affirm our life's mission: acknowledge where we did a good job, forgive ourselves where we've not done well, then marvel at what we have become as a living art-piece of God's work in us, with *lots of love to give yet!*

4. Connect/*re*connect with nature: enjoy the universe as God's Scripture of Creation, be open to its mysteries, and see ourselves as vitally connected to it.

5. Enlarge our boundaries: stretch ourselves to do new things which stimulate us, physically, mentally, emotionally, socially and spiritually, so we can affirm and expand our gifts of intuition, feeling, intellect, and sensation.

6. Enrich and nurture our personal potential: develop a talent, hobby or skill, not for money (though it may come), but for personal satisfaction.

7. Become life's healers: let go of past hurts; forgive God, self, others and even the world; be healers of Mother Earth; pray for intergenerational healing, and let any negative emotions/hurts stop with us so they'll not be passed on. (As we choose peace and love within, peace and love will radiate out from us.)

8. <u>Become builders of a legacy</u>: ask, "What shall we leave unto the 7th generation"? (A Native American Tradition) This one we'll never see.

9. <u>Stand open</u>: plan for our next decade of life as we focus on what we *can do* rather on what we can't/won't do; possibilities are endless, if we *want* to change.

10. <u>Deepen our friendship with Christ</u>: discover new ways of relating to him; we try new forms, and can't be tied to doing what we've always done. We can't grow spiritually if we hang on to methods which no longer feed us.

IV. We need to work at making the most of life and to enjoy the challenges that our rich, maturing process brings, even though there are many uncertain areas. We remember that life is a mystery to be lived, not a problem to be solved. (Rilke)

A. Society views aging as a disease, a period of inevitable decline, instead of seeing it as a transition which holds the possibility of being a rich and possibly the most fruitful time of life. Physical weakness does not mean spiritual weakness. In fact, it is through physical weakness that the spirit can actually become stronger.

1. Every person has physical weaknesses at each stage in life; yet, these are not equated with diminishment of any other aspects of the person--physical, mental, spiritual, or intellectual--except with reference to older people.

2. One of the secrets of eldering is to accept our age *at each age where we are.* In this way, we can make the most of our life and *enjoy* the journey of maturing slowly over time--like an old Giant Redwood tree that still bears seed, gives shade, and leaves a legacy of growth for the future.

a. We will ***not*** emphasize diminishments as the essence of our personhood and personality and see only decline and uselessness in these, at the expense of our ongoing, burgeoning strengths, talents and deepening love.

B. Ours is a *life-cycle*; for the first time in the history of the world, we can see it as such and make predictions about where we can go and about our choices as to how to get there. As we mature toward becoming a spiritual-elder-sage, ours can be ***Generation Wisdom!*** *("Aging is inevitable; maturing is optional.")*

1. We do not see ourselves as over-the-hill, nor under it, but *on top of it*, so we can see farther than we ever could before. Both our dreams and visions sharpen.

2. Some life-giving tasks we need to work at are to:

    a. Keep curiosity alive and be a lifelong learner.

    b. Safeguard independence, though we remain interdependent.

    c. Volunteer in some way and help those who need us.

    d. Work to change the image of older people in church and society.

    e. Keep a sense of humor and not take life so seriously.

    f. Take criticism lightly but not personally.

    g. Be open to love and to being loved as we find creative ways to do this.

    h. Greet each new day with grateful joy and let worries and anxieties go.

    i. Deepen friendship with Christ in creative, different ways in times of quiet.

    j. Have a plan and purpose in life, recall it often, and change it as needed.

V. Church communities need to take a creative look as to how they can enrich, enable, ennoble and empower older members through the decade-transitions. Parishes do reach out to needy members, but do very little to help active elders with personal growth.

    A. Statistics ('04) show that the majority of expendable parish money goes to children and teens; less than 1% is allocated to the development of adult members.

        1. Often, because of this imbalance, a great gap exists in meaningful rapport between younger and older members; there are few planned inter-group activities.

    B. Each decade of life needs to be ritualized in the parish. Since the older members are the wisdom-keepers, they need to be involved in other ways then with only giving money and volunteering. Their wisdom and spirituality must be given enriching opportunities and venues. Ritualizing the decades of transitions in community helps.

        1. Younger people need the mentoring and wisdom of the older parishioners; older members need the enthusiasm for life shown by the younger ones. Together, this intergenerational interaction is vital to the life of the parish and its people.

C. As we elder gracefully, we are ready to find new love. *Our best is just beginning!*

    1. Only *love* keeps people young at heart; as long as we choose to love, we'll never get old. We'll always have a lot of love to give, and when we choose *love*, we choose *life*. With both of these values permeating our spirit, our lives will be fruitful, full, and blest.

Some Questions to Ponder: Enabling Growth Through Transitions Unto Transformation

1. What is your attitude toward 'aging' in general?

2. What is your attitude toward your own eldering process?

3. What word or phrase word comes to mind when visualize an older man? An older woman? Your friends as older? Your parents?

4. What word or phrase comes when you visualize yourself as *older*?

5. How do you see your 'past as prologue' to your present and future life? How do you view the eldering process *as life's greatest educator*?

6. What is society's image of aging? How can you help to change it?

7. What image of aging does the institutional church usually have?

8. What are some biblical images of aging? Can you identify with someone?

9. What do the following words mean to you: aging, elder, eldering, senior, old, sage, spiritual-elder-sage? Do one or more of them hold a more positive image for you?

10. What other word(s) speak to you in a positive way about getting older? Which one(s) give you an uplift, and help formulate your life-vision?

11. How do you know when YOU are old? Or, don't you intend to get old?

12. Who were the older people in your life as you grew up; how did they affect your view of getting older, and of older people in general? How did their example influence you then and now?

13. What is your attitude and vision regarding older adult ministry?

14. Do you believe that you can always be *youthful*, if not young? What is the difference? What resolves can you make to gain a more informed view of the eldering process? How can you put this into practice? (Is the *best* yet to be?)

15. What do you see as God's ultimate purpose in your life? Granted that your commitment to Christ is non-negotiable, do you see that the *way* your commitment is lived out can change (even radically) during later life? How?

List other questions you have about the eldering process. Use them for further reflections on your journey through transitions unto transformation as you grow into a spiritual-elder-sage.

Some Scripture Quotes:
To Affirm Growth in the Maturing Process

1. "They that hope in the Lord will renew their strength, they will soar as with eagle's wings; they will run and not grow weary, walk and not grow faint." (Is 40:31)

2. "Truly you have formed my inmost being; you knit me in my mother's womb. I give you thanks that I am fearfully, wonderfully made..." (Ps 139:13-14)

3. "Then God said: 'Let us make man in our image, after our likeness.'" (Gn 1:26)

4. "Even to your old age I am the same, even when your hair is gray I will bear you; it is I who have done this, I will continue, and I who will carry you to safety." (Is 46:4)

5. "Then your life shall be brighter than the noonday; its gloom shall become as the morning, and you shall be secure because there is hope." (Jb 11:17)

6. "So with old age is wisdom, and with length of days understanding. With him are wisdom and might; his are counsel and understanding." (Jb 12:12-13)

7. "The glory of young men is their strength, and the dignity of old men is gray hair." (Prv 20:29)

8. "Cast me not off in my old age; as my strength fails, forsake me not." (Ps 71:9)

9. "O God, you have taught me from my youth, and till the present I proclaim your wondrous deeds; and now that I am old and gray, forsake me not till I proclaim your strength to every generation that is to come." (Ps 71:17-18)

10. "By me your days will be multiplied and the years of your life increased." (Prv 9:11)

11. "How blest are the poor in spirit; the reign of God is theirs...blest are they who hunger and thirst for holiness: they shall have their fill." (Mt 5:3,6)

Find some Scripture quotes which speak to your heart at this time of life.

Step 2: Relying on Christ's Power to Change

Came to believe that a Power greater that ourselves could restore us to sanity.

We come to believe that Christ's power in us can effect creative, positive change during our maturing process if we let him empower us in new ways.

Promise 2: We will not regret the past nor wish to shut the door on it.

We'll open new doors and walk with spiritual wellness into the future.

****

I. The second most important aspect of our maturing process over which *we have control* is our spiritual growth. A *positive attitude* to *choose Christ's higher energy* comes first, and must be the foundation for this second step to mature and bear fruit.

    A. Our spiritual growth and the changes it necessitates during major transitions in life are the bedrock for further development in this stage of our journey.

        1. People often stagnate at this spiritual level. They are afraid to change prayer-forms of previous levels of personal growth because of duty, routine, an attitude of have to, or, because of superimposed/or other-imposed shoulds and oughts.

        2. Perceived risks are involved in trying something new in our relationship with Christ. How do we know *what* Christ wants us to do? We just follow our heart.

    B. In Step Two, we continue our growth-progress as we accept our powerlessness to change the fact that we are growing older. We recognize our need for Christ during life's transitions in a new way. Only he can effect positive change.

        1. We need Christ in order to transform our thinking and our behavior. Our attempts to control and manage our eldering-process is out of our hands, but can and must be placed squarely in his.

            a. We need Christ's enabling and ennobling Presence and the power of the Spirit, to guide us creatively through the transitions of our eldering.

        2. We make a firm personal commitment to Christ to do our part to deepen friendship with him. We believe that he is our Power and strength in our eldering.

a. As with any meaningful relationship, deepening the one with Christ will take time. Reading, reflecting on his Word, watching videos, walking with him (as to Emmaus), and asking him to reveal himself to us both in new and ordinary ways are great helps. We have grown beyond our first love to a new level of intimacy and friendship.

b. Believing in Christ's power within us, and in our lives, requires faith *in him,* not in our skills and strengths; we let go and let Christ **be** *for us!*

II. As Christ matured, he too needed affirmation for his life's journey and ministry. The Father gave it: "This is my beloved Son. My favor rests on him." (Mt. 3:17)

A. The Father affirmed Christ's belovedness and life; he affirms ours, too. Even if we never actually heard the words with our ears, they are alive within us.

1. Each of us can say, *"I am a beloved son/daughter of God."* In this lies our journey of wellness. Our Higher Power has affirmed this truth in us. We grow.

2. God spoke this truth to us through someone who transmitted this message of belovedness. This is how we know God's love; human love is a conduit for God's.

3. We can only receive the gift of our belovedness through the love of others; we can only release another's belovedness through the gift of our love for them.

B. We release one another's belovedness, chosenness, beauty, radiance and preciousness, through, with and in Christ, by giving mutual affirmation, genuine compliments, esteem and respect. We both give and receive this gift.

1. We each must claim this, live it and keep aware of it, as the Light around us. The Power greater than ourselves is God, and God's love for us, through Christ.

2. The Lord called me from birth, from my mother's womb he gave me my name," (Is 49:1), which is 'beloved.' We, in turn, need to choose and internalize this truth, and to celebrate it in new ways during our life's transitions.

a. We listen with gratitude when others affirm this precious gift in us.

b. Gratefulness is next to being great; gratitude begets gratitude; love begets love; belovedness begets belovedness; radiance begets radiance.

3. As we mature, Christ's love in us grows. If we claim this love as *the* focus of our maturing years, our love will deepen. Love is simply for loving, and for no other reason. If we choose love, and affirm our belovedness, we become that which we have chosen and will have lots of love to give in our later years.

    a. We will be able to affirm these gifts in others who are a part of our lives.

C. When we choose to love another person, we become aware of their unique beauty, goodness, and belovedness. Within this love, we are energized to share the wonder of love which Christ is sharing with us with the whole world.

    1. With Christ at our love's controls, belovedness begets belovedness. We claim the truth of love growing within us, interiorize it, and walk tall in the awareness that we are chosen. On this reality, we build our transition years.

    2. All deep friendships--our mutual one with Christ, as well as friendships we have with others as an overflow of his love in us--call forth one another's beauty, preciousness, sacredness and belovedness. This higher energy is what cements and sacramentalizes our relationships, and allows us to walk in wellness.

III. Christ, our Power, has called us to renew our life in a unique way during our wisdom-framing years. "Then I heard the voice of the Lord saying: 'Whom shall I send? Who will go for us'? 'Here I am,' I said; 'Send me!' And he replied: 'Go.' " (Is 6:8-9)

    A. We have been chosen as the beloved one of the Father and have surrendered to this choice. We have then taken on the awesome task of being willing to be sent as a prophet to speak with positive attitudes and visions during our eldering years.

        1. Because of Christ, our Power, we have a *response-ability* to let him energize, empower and enable us to have a positive outlook. His Power in us restores us to youthful creativity and spiritual balance. <u>*Being restored to balance and sanity is being restored to love; being restored to love, is being restored to both.*</u>

        2. He's with us: "You are mine whom I have chosen...you, whom I have called my servant...fear not, I am with you; be not dismayed; I am your God. I will strengthen you, and help you...you shall rejoice in the Lord." (Is 41:8-10,16)

B. We look at Christ and believe in his power, a power greater than ourselves. He loves us so much that he only wants us to love. He went to be with his Father, but because of love, he remains with us in the Eucharist "even unto the end of time," through all of our life's transitions, unto our transformation of loving eternally.

    1. We are his new *bread* and *wine*, chosen to carry and give his life, love, light, and presence to our world, in our own dynamic ways, at *this time* in life.

    2. We are *offered, consecrated* and given for *communion* as living Eucharists. We take Christ's love and presence, in *our* love and presence, to the world, through, with, and in him in creative, innovative ways at *this time* of life.

C. In this transition time of life, **_We are Offered:_** lifted and broken as the grains of wheat which make the bread, given to become a radiant Christ-presence in the world.

    1. We offer ourselves daily, imperfect and broken as we are, to the Father, through, with, and in Christ, so that we may become fresh bread for him to bless, consecrate, and give in communion to a Christ-starved world.

    2. We offer our belovedness, his first gift to us. We make this offering in our 'yes,' (*Fiat,* Latin*)* and 'wow,' (*Magnificat*, Latin, a 'celebration') because he has done great things *to, with, in, and through us* to change the world around us.

D. In this transition time of life, **_We are Consecrated:_** blest, and able to bless because of consecration, though we feel as crushed as the grapes which make the wine.

    1. In our very offering we yield to consecration. We await Christ's touch quietly, for his sacred touch affirms our own belovedness; he irradiates us with love.

    2. Our 'yes' joins Christ's and creates the very reality of which it speaks, our own consecration. Within this consecration, we too can consecrate; we take time to be aware of this incredible gift, claim it, and share it wherever we can.

        a. Blessing begets blessing; consecration begets consecration. What we receive, we are meant to give; what we give, we will receive yet more. In the blessing and the consecration, we release one another's belovedness. Because of consecration, we believe that we have 'lots of love to give yet.'

E. In this transition time of life, ***We are given in Communion:*** we have *offered* ourselves; we have been *consecrated.* We stand open and ready to be given in *communion* to a world which is starving for the Presence of the Risen Christ, coming to it through, with, and in us. In this love lies our sanity and spirituality.

    1. The most challenging, yet exciting wisdom time of life lies ahead of us as we surrender it to 'our Higher Power,' Christ. Our life's greatest fulfillment lies in being able to give ourselves in love. As we do so, we become ever more beautiful in our belovedness, and what we give is beautiful: *our unique love.*

    2. If we do not give such sacred love, unique and non-repeatable, we shall die with our love cooped up, and with our original, awesome, unsung love song still locked within our hearts. The world will be a poorer place because of it.

IV. As we let Christ be our Power, we become living conduits of his life, love, light, and presence. Because of our deepening friendship with Christ, we change our own attitudes toward eldering. We become catalysts for change in church and society.

    A. Intimacy is the goal of communion. As we surrender to new intimacy with Christ, it's not possible to separate lover and beloved. The two radiate from one another, complement one another, and are always active in one another's lives. These realities are enfleshed in every thought, word, action, gift, and use of talent.

    B. We're made for eternal transformation: to be Eucharist-lovers for the world through our unique love. Let's be ready to give it; someone will be waiting!

        1. As we recognize our vocation of being called to love, we believe that Christ's Power in us can effect creative, positive change during our eldering years. Because of this, we will walk with sanity, balance, and spiritual wellness into our eldering.

Some Questions to Ponder:
Enabling Growth Through Transitions Unto Transformation

1. How do you witness to the fact that you are a 'beloved of God'? Be specific.

2. How does Christ's Power in you effect change in you when you feel powerless?

3. What are some areas of your life where you have difficulty believing that you are a 'beloved of God'? How can you be more aware, and really walk tall in this belief?

4. If your relationship with Christ was given as a weather report, how would it read?

5. How do you think Christ might be using this transformation time in your life to open something new for you, something you have only dreamed of, but thought could never happen? (Or, something so new/different that you never even dreamed of it?) Are you happy? Anxious? Afraid? Uncertain? Thrilled? Excited? Apprehensive?

6. How can surrendering to Christ as your *personal* Higher-Power make a real difference in this transition time of life? What image can illustrate your being his 'conduit'?

7. How, with Christ's help, can you make necessary changes in your life so that the present maturing process will be more creative and life-giving for you? What might *he* be wanting to teach you through this process? At this time in your life journey?

8. No one can manage life alone; yet, with Christ, all things are possible. What are some things you still think are impossible for you that you need to surrender *now?* Itemize areas where you specifically need Christ's help to move forward and grow.

9. Are you ready to be restored to a positive view (sanity/balance) of your eldering process? How can you make necessary changes so you no longer see aging as a 'disease'?

10. Who has transmitted The Father's love and a sense of your belovedness to you? To whom have you transmitted God's love and a sense of belovedness?

11. What symbols (not religious ones) speak to you of Christ's Power in your life?

12. We need to feed ourselves with positive images (as Christ did) so we will be able to affirm our belovedness. What are the positive images you have of yourself? (I am---)

13. Mary's two words (Fiat/'yes' and Magnificat/'wow') framed her surrender to Christ's life in and through her. What words frame yours, especially at this transition time?

14. What are some new doors you can open in order to walk with spiritual wellness into the future of your next part of life, so as to make it full of Christ's higher energy?

List other questions you have about the eldering process. Use them for further reflections on your journey through transitions unto transformation as you grow into a spiritual-elder-sage.

Some Scripture Quotes:
To Affirm Growth in the Maturing Process

1. When we've completed life's transitions and have reached full maturity, we will hear: "Well done, my beloved son/daughter...you have my Father's blessing...come, inherit the kingdom I've prepared for you from the foundation of the world." (Mt 25:21,34)

2. "I will never forget you. See, upon the palms of my hands I have written your name." (Is 49:15-16)

3. "Anyone who did accept him he empowered to become children (beloved) of God." (Jn 1:12)

4. "I assure you, if you had faith the size of a mustard seed, you would be able to say to this mountain 'Move from here to there,' and it would move. Nothing would be impossible for you." (Mt 17:20)

5. "Here is my beloved...my chosen one, with whom I am well pleased...upon whom I have put my Spirit...I have grasped you by the hand...I formed you, and set you as a covenant of the people, a light for the nations...to open the eyes of the blind, to bring out prisoners from confinement, and from the dungeon, those who live in darkness." (Is 42:1,6,7)

6. "We can be sure that God is with us and that we will receive at his hands whatever we ask. Why? Because we are keeping his commandments and doing what is pleasing in his sight. His commandment is this: we are to believe in the name of his son, Jesus Christ, and are to love one another as he commanded us." (1 Jn 21-23)

7. "Fear not, I am with you; be not dismayed; I am your God. I will strengthen you and help you, and uphold you with my right hand..." (Is 41:10)

8. "Jesus asked him, 'What do you want me to do for you?' 'Rabboni,' the blind man said, 'I want to see.' Jesus said in reply, 'Be on your way. Your faith has healed you.' Immediately he received his sight and started to follow him up the road."(Mk 10:51-52)

9. "Jesus said to him 'If you can'? Everything is possible to one who trusts.' The boy's father immediately exclaimed, 'I do believe! Help my lack of trust!' " (Mk 9:23-24)

10. "Then I heard the voice of the Lord saying, 'Whom shall I send? Who will go for us?' 'Here I am; ' I said; 'send me.' And he replied, 'Go!' " (Is 6:-9)

11. "My entire being is ready to burst with the joy of the Lord. My spirit has stroked the radiant face of God. For God has looked upon me in my brokenness and weakness;

yet, he has called me to be a   brilliant light to his people. The Lord God has done in credibly wonderful things to me, magnificent is his name." (Lk 1:46-49) (Adapted: Angelita)

Find some Scripture quotes which speak to your heart at this time of life.

Step 3:Surrendering To Christ

Made a decision to turn our will and our lives over
to the care of God as we understood him.

We make a firm decision to turn our eldering process over to Christ, and to whatever new love and life he has in store for us at this time of life.

<u>Promise 3:</u> We will comprehend the word serenity and we will know peace.

We'll know peace and serenity as we let ourselves be 'clothed with Christ.'

****

I. Real success in life, external and internal, requires both *passion* and *vision;* turning our life over to Christ takes *both* at a radical level. Being 'clothed with Christ' is the reason we were created; taking his love and presence to the world, is our life's goal.

A. Once we turn our life over to the care of Christ, he asks two important changes:

1. That we be willing to *let go* of old, set ways so that we can be open to new ways of loving and living that he will show us.

2. That we be ready to open our heart and *believe* that, as we are clothed with Christ, we have *lots of love to give yet.* In this lies our peace and serenity.

B. We craft our own eldering transitions. We began this crafting as soon as we met older persons in our life. Did we want to grow up and be like them, or did we learn what not to do in our own maturing as we watched them?

1. Our spirit is as young as when God first created it; we get older, but we do not have to get *old.* Getting old is an attitude of mind, made that way by negative self-messages, or by accepting those superimposed by others.

a. We let go of some things and take on others that fit us *now* and are life-giving; *we do not* focus on *can't do's, but on **can do's.***

C. We need to discard role identity as the moving force on our lives. We are more than our role--even Paul of Tarsus had to find that out as he discarded the old.

1. We work at differentiating between *roles* and who we really *are* as persons. The two are distinctly separate; we must find a life beyond our role. Previously, roles lasted as long as a person's life because of the brief lifecycle.

Today, we need to discard these 'old clothes' to find hidden love and talents.

II. As we become 'clothed with Christ,' we remember that love is simply for loving and for nothing else. It is the reason Christ came: "I came to bring fire to earth, and what would I but that it be kindled." (Lk 12:49) and " I came that they might have life and have it abundantly." (Jn 10:10) These two hold Christ's Vision-Quest-Commitment.

    A. In being more open to Christ's energy in our lives, we find that *love* is the *only virtue* that can guide us through our transitions. We recognize this and are ready to formulate our own vision-quest-commitment for the next stage of our maturing.

        1. Generally, we've not been taught *how* to love. Fear gets in the way, since the opposite of love is *fear*, not hate. Christ will replace our fears with love.

        2. In our surrender, we face two fundamental affirmations especially during our transitions in life: *God's love*, and his will for us to have *life* in abundance, and *our life's goal* to develop more fully this life and love in us during our eldering.

        3. In these two strengths, life and love, we strongly affirm the *now*, the present moment. We learn to see love and beauty all around us, and all ground as sacred.

    B. Our gift of life is the supreme gift of God's love. Our only purpose is to live this life abundantly by being clothed with the love of the greatest lover, Christ, and then to take his life and love to the world in whatever way possible. We do this especially during our wisdom-touched years in ways we never could have before.

        1. This abundance of life within us, this quality of our living, is only made possible in and through our relationships with God, self, others and world. *God is love, and his will for us is to have life and love in abundance. That's all!*

        2. We 'live Christ,' and slowly come to see God's love and beauty everywhere. We'll see suffering and hear cries for help where we never noticed before, but, we'll also discover (and give) love and compassion in the least likely of places. Our vision-quest will be re-created, and our commitment to it will be stronger because we are at last *beginning* to love. Chardin pointed out that "when the world truly discovers love, it will have discovered fire for the second time."

III. We turn our lives over to Christ, and see that our next stage is not an inevitable fate, nor a disease. It's a grace-filled time wherein personal growth incredibly matures.

A. In our maturing, we reflect on what can be done with the new life, abundant love, and Christ-centered energies that are newly surfacing, and our will is one with his. We let go of the old garments of our self-centered control, and stand open to Christ's care of our lives. This way, we are 'clothed with him' anew right *now*.

    1. We need to *remember, integrate, do a life-review, and reminisce* in order to see how Christ's hand has been on our shoulder every step of our way. Then we need to formulate a legacy that we can leave unto the 7th Generation.

B. These activities serve as catapults for a fresh, creative sense of direction in this potentially fruitful time of life. They help us to let go of pining for the 'good old times' when we could ??, and instead, to see the good times as the <u>now</u>-times.

    1. We remember the *past* to enrich the *present* and to set a course for the *future* with our learned wisdom, spiritual growth, and repaired mistakes.

C. By turning our lives over to Christ for our eldering process, there are tasks to do:

    1. <u>We ask ourselves three main questions</u>: (1) to what have I given **life**; (2) to what have I given **love**; and (3) what am I leaving as my **legacy?**

        a. Leaving a *legacy* is as vital as giving *life* and *love*. A generation which doesn't remember, respect, and appreciate its past is doomed to repeat its mistakes. It has no foundation on which to build its future hopes, dreams, visions, love, life and faith. *We* turn our lives over to Christ and are loving foundation-builders of the future.

        b. Others need to know our stories in order to create their own. A feeling of rootedness is essential to a dynamic, fruitful, healthy, spiritual life.

2. <u>We pray more, tell family/personal stories</u>. We laugh often, sing songs, are tender toward children, take long walks, and experience God's Scripture of creation. Daily, we think of, or write down, ten things for which to thank God.

3. <u>We review our lives</u>. We make sense of our 'failures,' and see them now as necessary steps to spiritual maturing. These are not junk to be discarded, but are fertilizer for new fruitfulness in our next transition. We choose life!

4. <u>We keep saying to ourselves</u> (with Robert Browning): "Grow old along with me, the best is yet to be, the last of life for which the first was made."

5. <u>We discard the concept that we 'have to get old.'</u> We get *older* as does a baby, but our attitude keeps our spirit as young as when God first created us.

6. Our eldering process comes alive in the sacredness of the ordinary. As we stand before Christ daily and let ourselves be clothed with him, our inner strength becomes a radiant light which carries life and love to all around us.

7. We work to change the view of aging in both church and society. We change it from one of non-productive consumers who are 'takers,' to one of enablement and empowerment wherein older people are seen as having lots of love to give, much lived wisdom, and many talents to use for church and society.

8. We work to discover spiritual depths not uncovered. We have love not yet discovered. We share life's lived wisdom, generate energy, enable life, empower love and become a light-filled conduit for Christ's life of abundance.

9. We grow in wisdom, we grieve and mourn better for losses. We accept more peacefully our own, and others' limitations. There is grace in each transition-loss. This is not a single event, but a pattern of surrender. It is a cycle of loss/gain by letting go. It is purification for being 'clothed with Christ.'

10. We look at ourselves in the mirror each morning and smile at God. We thank God for making us so handsome/beautiful and full of Christ. We greet God with a new 'yes,' and ask for the Spirit's help in taking Christ's life, love, light and presence to the world today--so he can change it through us.

IV. As we turn our eldering transitions over to Christ, we need to set a clear focus by formulating a *Vision-Quest-Commitment* statement if the 'last of life' is to be our best.

A. We gain a vision of our maturing potential from elders/mentors in our lives. We sift out what we have learned and create a focus for our later life. Our Vision-Quest-Commitment statement summarizes and focuses our Christ-centered energy for the next part of our lives. What does this mean, and how do we create one?

1. *Our Vision* is comprised of several elements: physical, emotional, mental, social, and spiritual. Our will shapes our vision through:

    a. Awareness.

    b. Goal setting.

    c. A plan of action.

    d. Stick-to-it-tivity.

    e. Much courage.

    f. Daily quiet time with Christ in prayer to ponder our life's transitions.

2. _Our Quest_ gives wings to our vision and makes it do-able; it helps us discover different ways to live out our vision in daily life. It keeps us focused, balanced, and open to new ideas. It is the daily search for ways to channel our energies toward the fulfillment of our vision, and takes place deep within us.

3. _Our Commitment_ implies a consecration *by* God and *to* God of our life, our love, our changing ministry, and our reason for living. It is a kind of ordination to work toward the fulfillment of our vision through our quest. It is a covenant to live our years fully as God's beloved one 'with fire in our belly!'

    a. We need to: write down to whom our commitment is made (not to an institution, but to a *person,* for us, Christ), and use energetic verbs to specifically describe the action to take place and the group we'll serve.

B. Our Vision-Quest-Commitment needs to be clear, with room for growth:

It must:

    1. Use present tense as if it is already happening; we become what we envision.

    2. Be able to cover all life's activities: personal, spiritual, communal, work, leisure, social, etc.; our loving spirit expresses itself in all of these areas.

    3. Be specific; generalities do not work.

    4. Be brief to be easily remembered; the shorter the better.

    5. Be visible; seeing it daily is a great help.

    6. Be daily turned over to Christ for blessing; taking it to him in prayer helps.

C. Surrendering to Christ anew in our maturing years is a transition full of uncertainty and loss, but there's potential for incredible, never-experienced growth.

D. The _Fall_ of our lives is richer than _Spring_ if we are aware of our potential. We will gather the fruits of our _Summer_ labors so that the _Winter_ of later life will be fruitful, because _our harvest is reaped, stored, and ready to be shared._

Some Questions to Ponder:
Enabling Growth through Transitions
Unto Transformation

1. What are some 'old garments' in the closet of my set ways that I need to get rid of so that I may be clothed anew with Christ and turn the care of my transitions over to him? What is my greatest fear about turning my maturing years over to Christ?

2. How can I define myself, my personhood, in other ways besides by role or ministry?

3. How can I share love, life and lived wisdom with others at *this* transition time of life?

4. What can I do now that I've never had the time or courage to do before? Do I believe that Christ is truly in control of my new life, and that I *can* move ahead with his help?

5. What are some worrisome things in my transitions that I need to surrender to Christ, so that this present stage of my life can be more positive, loving, giving and hopeful?

6. As I reflect on my past life, what love/s can I celebrate? Which ones have transformed my life? Earlier? Now? Could do so in the future?

7. How often do I spend quiet time with Christ so I may receive his life in abundance? How can I be more conscious of Christ's love so as to let this love radiate from me?

8. To what have I given *life*? To what have I given *love*? What can I leave as *legacy*?

9. What kind of a life-filled, loving person have I become through my maturing? Who are/have been my love heroes, my love mentors? How can **I** mentor love?

10. In what ways am letting myself be 'clothed with Christ'? How am I giving him the care of my maturing process, so that his *life* and *love* may flow through me *now?*

11. Since I'll not 'play God' any more, and I'm not sure where this new part of my journey will take me, what can I let go of as I trust Christ to lead me on?

List other questions you have about the eldering process. Use them for further reflections on your journey through transitions unto transformation as you grow into a spiritual-elder-sage.

Some Scripture Quotes:
To Affirm Growth in the Maturing Process

1. "Trust in the Lord with all your heart, on your own intelligence rely not; in all your ways be mindful of him, and he will make straight you paths." (Prv 3:5-6)

2. "We know that God makes all things work together for the good of those who love him who have been called according to his decree. Those whom he foreknew he predestined to share the image of his Son..." (Rom 8:28-29)

3. "I continually thank my God for you because of the favor he has bestowed on you in Christ Jesus, in whom you have been richly endowed with every gift of speech and knowledge." (1 Cor 1:4-5)

4. "Turning your ear to wisdom, inclining your heart to understanding; yes, if you call to intelligence, and to understanding raise your voice...then will you understand the fear of the Lord; the knowledge of God you will find." (Prv 2:2)

5. "Follow the way prescribed for you by the Lord, your God, that you may live and prosper, and may have a long life in the land which you are to occupy." (Dt 5:33)

6. "I will deliver him and glorify him; with length of days I will gratify him and will show him my salvation." (Ps 91:16)

7. "By me your days will be multiplied and the years of your life increased." (Prv 9:11)

8. "Let me know, O Lord, my end and what is the number of my days, that I may learn how frail I am." (Ps 39:5)

9. "He must increase, I must decrease." (Jn 3:30)

10. "You have been consecrated in Christ Jesus and called to be a holy people...you are Christ's and Christ is God's." (1 Cor 1:2; 3:23)

11. "Jesus, for his part, progressed steadily in wisdom, age and grace before God and humankind." (Lk 2:52)

12. "It is no longer I who live, but Christ who lives in me." (Gal 2:20)

13. "Come, follow me." (Mt 19:21)

14. "Speak, Lord, your servant is listening." (Sm 3:10)

15. "If Christ is in you, then your very spirit is life itself." (Rom 8:10-11)

Find some Scripture quotes which speak to your heart at this time of life.

Step 4: Taking Personal Inventory

Made a searching and fearless moral inventory of ourselves.

We make a searching, fearless inventory regarding our maturing process. Through this inventory, we'll learn more about our eldering time of life in order to grow through transitions unto greater spiritual transformation.

<u>Promise 4</u>: No matter how far down the scale we have gone, we will see how our experience can benefit others.

We'll accept our past, and let our experience and wisdom benefit others.

****

I. In order to be fruitful, all eldering is essentially one of spiritual growth and positive inner change. We anticipate each transition as a challenge to grow in wisdom.

A. Taking a positive inventory regarding our maturing process, and making an effort to learn more about it, will help us know how to create our next transition.

1. We may not just let aging happen; we must absolutely plan for each transition, through each gain/loss cycle unto transformation.

2. Transitions are indispensable. They involve adjustments; they often find us unprepared; they are difficult; they do not wait for us to approve. Without them, there is no maturing. Afterwards, we're no longer the same.

B. In transitions, something is ending and must be let go. Old motivations no longer carry us through. Enthusiasm seems to have waned. We are indifferent to things that once challenged us, and our focus begins to wander.

1. We are called to say *good-by* to one stage of life before we know what the next one will be. We've done this as a child, a teen and a young adult. Why should we be more anxious about transitions during our more mature years?

2. Two emotions surface within us: one says *to resist,* the other calls us *to strive.* We must let go of the past, so that something new can be born *now.*

C. Taking inventory asks: what does God want of me at this time of life, and how can integration, simplicity and singleness of purpose help to get rid of nonessentials?

1. Both of these transition questions are based on love and call us to new love. Our many losses/transitions simply prepare us for transformation. They help to sift-out ('crisis') what is nonessential and lead us to what is important *now*.

2. In each of these potentially growth-filled transitions, we are searching for the core meaning in our lives. The difficult part is the darkness and/or emptiness that accompany these stages. *We don't know how to be the age we are, and what is required of us as we take a fearless inventory of our eldering process.*

> **a.** At earlier transitions, others could predict losses for us; we had an idea of what was in store, even though we had to muddle through in our own way.

> **b.** During our more responsible eldering years, we have had no such support; however, the present longevity-factor studies can afford some predictions.

3. Some transitions are predictable, others, are not. It's 'what we do with what we have that counts.' There are some practical activities which help us to take a fearless moral (*correctness of behavior*) inventory for our eldering process.

II. Through our inventory, a resurrection of spirit will take place. In our transition process, we know *new life* is happening. Rolling that old stone away is the problem

> **A.** As with Christ's resurrection, *he* is the one to roll back the stone. He *will* roll back our 'stone' if we do our part, through inventory, to be open to new possibilities. Some important activities we can do to get ready for this 'rolling' are to:

> > **1.** Create alone-time to do 'homework' in this area. Frequent periods of solitude will permit us to keep our appointment with Christ so that he can touch us with his love, light, life and presence to enlighten our eldering pathway.

> > **2.** Set aside a longer period of quiet time weekly for reflection. Through this we'll discover many new ways Christ is using to 'rolling the stone' away.

> > **3.** Reflect on the fact that Christ saved the best wine until last. We'll search to change and/or enrich our attitude with ideas regarding the eldering process.

> > **4.** Make time daily just to sit with Christ and ask him to touch us deeply inside. We'll ask him to heal what needs healing, to shine his light on our inventory process, and to support and guide us as we make major decisions for this time of life.

5. <u>Write</u> our autobiography to include all dimensions of our journey, inner and outer. This helps us make our moral inventory by reframing/reviewing our lives.

6. <u>Find or make</u> a sacred space where we can go *to pray*, i.e., *to reflect* on our relationship with Christ. Ask his help to find the mission he yet wants us to do.

7. <u>Formulate</u> our own creed as a spiritual-elder-sage, pray it often, and change it when necessary. State it in first person so that our dreams will happen: (a) "I believe that a spiritual-elder-sage is a person who---;" and (b) "I believe that as a spiritual-elder-sage, I am --, I can --, I will---."

8. <u>Create</u> a sacred life-pouch and place in it three non-perishable items which speak of our life's journey. This can be passed on as legacy or buried with us.

9. <u>Craft</u> our own eldering by imaging ourselves at various transitions in life. We imagine how our love, talents and spirituality will be developed expressed.

10. <u>Seek</u> reliable resources to assist our maturing process. Libraries, book-stores, videos, tapes, retreats, workshops, courses, etc., all help.

11. <u>Develop</u> a 'memory scrapbook' which could be an expansion of a family tree. However, we put more than a *dash* between birth and death to tell life's story!

12. <u>Keep</u> a journal and write in it daily to keep focused on what's really important during our various eldering transitions. Journalizing as a prayerform helps.

13. <u>Visualize</u> positive role models in older people. (List negative traits from some others so as to learn what *not* to become.) Being specific helps us to describe ourselves as we become a spiritual-elder-sage. We become what we image.

14. <u>Write letters</u> of appreciation to significant people who have helped us on life's journey. Let them know our gratitude, and that we are better persons because they have been part of our lives. If that someone is deceased, or never even known, we write a letter anyway, and keep it in our journal as a lodestone.

15. <u>Journalize</u> our life. Following are some helps toward maintaining a focus.

    a. <u>Include</u> what we perceive to be a pattern of our life. Dividing up life into decades helps; we include dreams, both filled and unfulfilled.

b. <u>Enclose pictures</u> of people who have influenced our life.

c. <u>State major turning points/transitions</u> in life and why they were important. We reflect on the grace they held, even if only recognized in hindsight.

d. <u>Contemplate</u> our *past* and consciously ponder the *present.* This way, we construct a *future* based on God's grace, self-knowledge, wisdom and growth.

e. <u>Write-out</u> specific insights about our friendship with Christ.

f. <u>Hold up</u> our unique, Christ-touched spiritual-elder-sage image. We revisit this image whenever we need it to encourage and affirm our growth.

16. <u>Pass-on</u> the stewardship of the world. Care of/for the universe rests on the shoulders of spiritual elders; it must be part of our legacy for next generation.

17. <u>Script</u> our last moments on earth in the most ideal, positive manner possible. This actually helps to anticipate our new life of transformation and not fear it.

18. <u>Outline</u> our Resurrection Service. It will be our 'coronation celebration!'

19. <u>Write</u> our obituary. Do an article for the parish bulletin and/or newspaper.

20. <u>Request</u> a special caption or motto for our gravestone. We make it complimentary/positive; no one can argue with us then! (We've got the last word!)

III. As we engage in the above activities, we will be making a 'fearless, moral inventory' and a deeply spiritual one. Both will enrich our later-life transitions.

A. Sometimes, a transition challenges us to move on, but not where we thought we were mapped-out to go. At other times, we are challenged to stay where we are, to grow where we've been planted, and to develop new roots with fresh, delicious fruit.

B. Through this inventory technique, we realize that a seemingly empty tomb is not an indication of death, but a prelude to the radiant possibilities of new life.

1. The focus of our lives can change if we make certain life-giving choices, and do all in our power to help make them into a reality. The inventory is very helpful; it gives us the tools, but we are the ones who must use them to create the eldering process that we want for ourselves.

2. From this new vantage point we can look back and look ahead like at no other time of life, as we use the wisdom we've gleaned over the years.

3. We have never been in a better place in life, or more ready to decide what we can create today, so that our tomorrows will be richer and more full of the love that is uniquely our own.

> **a.** "Life is either a great adventure or it is nothing at all." --Helen Keller

> **b.** "True life is lived when tiny changes occur." --Leo Tolstoy

> **c.** "Your future depends on many things, but mostly on you."—Frank Tyger

C. *As we do our inventory*, we remember several necessary principles. <u>We:</u>

1. Care for ourselves, and try to look our best at the age we are.

2. Nurture our spirituality in whatever way we can.

3. Repair our bodies daily by rest, diet, exercise, and learning.

4. Draw on life's experiences to affirm that we are wise, and growing in wisdom and grace before God and humankind.

5. Stay connected to friends, family and community as much as possible, and then reach out to serve or help them whenever and however we are able.

6. Try to see love and beauty all around us, to sense all ground as sacred, and begin to realize that *our* unique love is essential to creating love in the world.

7. Stay connected to Christ, our energy source of love and life, though our daily meditation and quiet prayer time.

8. Remember that *"Anyone who keeps the ability to see beauty never grows old."-- Frank Kafka.*

Some Questions to Ponder: Enabling Growth Through Transitions Unto Transformation

1. How have you made a fearless inventory of your own eldering process?

2. What is the image of yourself as a spiritual-eldering-sage? How do you feel about it?

3. What age would you be if you did not know the age you *are*?

4. Which of the activities suggested here do you think will be helpful at this time of life? Do you think that doing some of them will help to reframe your life and assist you in creating a fresh Vision-Quest-Commitment upon which to build your future?

5. In your transition stages, are you a *resister* or a *striver?* How do you know?

6. As you do the inventory, what adjustments are you willing to make so that the next transition can be even more positive than the last one?

7. How willing are you to say good-by to previous stages of life, even before you can fully formulate your vision for the next one? Are you willing to 'wing it'?

8. What 'stones' need rolling away so that new life can emerge for your next transition in life's journey? How can you use this inventory as an incentive to learn more about your resurrection time of life so that the last of life will really be the best?

9. How do you see the empty tomb of past transitions? As ones which merely describe death/loss, or as ones which are preludes to new life you never dreamed of?

10. How do you feel about journalizing? Will it be helpful to you? Why or why not? Would you be willing to try it for a few months to see if it would make a difference in the way you view your life's transitions? Might it help create new possibilities?

11. What else have you discovered about yourself at this new transition time of life?

List other questions you have about the eldering process. Use them for further reflections on your journey through transitions unto transformation as you grow into a spiritual-elder-sage.

Some Scripture Quotes: To Affirm Growth in the Maturing Process

1. "The Spirit too helps us in our weakness for we do not know how to pray as we ought; but the Spirit makes intercession for us with groanings that cannot be expressed in speech." (Rom 8:26)

2. "Let us search out and examine our ways that we may return to the Lord." (Lam 3:40)

3. " I have waited, waited for the Lord, and he stooped toward me and heard my cry. He drew me out of the pit of destruction, out of the mud of the swamp; he set my feet upon a crag; he made firm my steps...he put a new song into my mouth. (Ps 40:1-4)

4. "The Lord gives wisdom, from his mouth come knowledge and understanding; he has counsel in store for the upright, he is the shield of those who walk honestly." (Prv 2:6-7)

5. "Therefore I prayed, and prudence was given to me; I pleaded and the spirit of Wisdom came to me." (Wis 7:7)

6. "Rise up in splendor! Your light has come, the glory of the Lord shines upon you. See, darkness covers the earth, and thick clouds cover the peoples; but upon you the Lord shines, and over you appears his glory. Nations shall walk by your light, and kings by your shining radiance." (Is 60:1-3)

7. "The spirit of the Lord is upon me, because the Lord has anointed me; he has sent me to bring glad tidings to the lowly, to heal the brokenhearted, to proclaim liberty to the captives and to release the prisoners." (Is 61:1)

8. "The word of the Lord came to me thus: 'Before I formed you in the womb I knew you, before you were born I dedicated you, a prophet to the nations I appointed you.' 'Ah, Lord God,' I said, 'I know not how to speak; I am too young.' But the Lord answered me. 'Say not, I am too young. To whomever I send you, you shall go; whatever I command you, you shall speak. Have no fear before them, because I am with you to deliver you, says the Lord.' Then the Lord extended his hand and touched my mouth, saying, ' See, I place my words in your mouth!' " (Jer 1:5-9)

9. "Fear not, my children; call upon God, who will deliver you from oppression at enemy hands." (Bar 4:21)

10. "I came that they might have life and have it to the full." (Jn 10:10)

11. " As the Father has loved me, so I have loved you. Live on in my love... All this I tell you that my joy may be yours and your joy may be complete." (Jn 15: 9-11)

Find some Scripture quotes which speak to your heart at this time of life.

Step 5:Admitting Wrongs

Admitted to God, to ourselves, and to another human being the
exact nature of our wrongs.

*We admit to Christ, to ourselves, and to at least one trusted friend,
the struggles and failures we've experienced by refusing to learn about,
and to face, personal changes in this transition time of life.*

<u>Promise 5:</u> The feeling of uselessness and self-pity will disappear.

We'll experience freedom from feelings of uselessness and self-pity.

****

I. When we make no (or little) effort to learn about new life-transitions, we are closed to life-giving possibilities. We allow ourselves a downhill slide and see this as a degenerative time of life instead of one in which we still 'have lots of love to give.'

> **A.** "We cannot live in the afternoon of life according to the program of life's morning, for what was great in the morning will be little at evening, and what in the morning was true will at evening have become a lie." --Carl Jung
>
> > **1.** At no other time in the history of the world, especially in the US, has the longevity factor been able to be studied. With a large number of centenarians still living, and increasing daily, human growth and development can be studied in ways that never could have been done before.
> >
> > > **a.** We can now predict some essential elements of our maturing transitions. This was not possible just a few years ago, and by being able to anticipate changes, we can plan for them and find the ones we do have control over.
>
> **B.** In the big picture, it is wrong to stay stuck in past (comfortable?) ways of viewing our eldering process. That way, we don't have to do anything about it; we simply let life slide downhill as did previous, uninformed generations.
>
> > **1.** Once we admit that we need to get involved in our own transitions, we can no longer just sit back and let life happen *to* us. We have a responsibility to make life happen, according to our *informed* attitudes, desires and dreams.
> >
> > **2.** We need to admit to someone where we have taken the line of least effort. No matter how many years we have behind us (or how few), we need to start learning, or to broaden our base continually if we have already started.

47

II. The first step here is to admit that we have neither put forth sufficient effort to face this transition time of life--with all the creative changes that can take place--nor, have we really read or studied very much about our maturing growth-transitions. Kierkegaard said: "Life may be understood backward, but must be lived forward."

A. In Erikson's Stages of Life, he emphasizes *generativity* as the healthy trait of adulthood, with *self-absorption* as its opposite. Within this trait, *care*--and anything created or generated by *our love*--is the outstanding virtue.

1. As we move through our transitions, we merely add-on the next trait and accompanying virtue if our attitude and effort have been, and are, positive.

2. In what Erikson calls 'old age,' *integrity* is its trait, and *wisdom* the outstanding quality or virtue. *Despair* is given as its opposite. We must choose.

B. Once we realize that our aging process has been dictated by our own attitude, we must confess what that attitude is: positive or negative. Many people focus on what can *not* be done, instead of on what yet *can* be accomplished. We choose.

1. We must name our negative attitude out loud so that it does not keep setting up housekeeping in our spirit where it clouds our dreams and visions. We have to *say it* so we can actually hear it with our own ears: "I believe that getting older is---." Then, we can *know* where our attitude and effort are leading.

a. Also, we ask: "What am I'm doing with my life *now* to prepare for life's next transition? Am I am letting myself become a demanding, negative, self-centered, crotchety, *old* person, just because I'm getting older"?

b. What we will become as an older person is being created *now*; each new tomorrow we'll be older, but we never have to get old! My *attitude* governs my thoughts and actions today and creates each new tomorrow.

c. Children, filled with the excitement of always discovering something fresh each new year of life, cannot wait until their next birthday. Answering the question: "How old are you"?, they usually respond with their present age, but are quick to add: "But, I'm going to be--." (What has happened to *our* anticipation and excitement for living *our* next year?)

2. Children do not bemoan the losses of previous years; they let go of what they used to do and are thrilled about what they *can do now* that they could not do before. "When I was little, I used to ---; but, now, I -----!" (Even if being 'little' was just last year when they were four!) What about the child in us?

C. All life is made up of losses; until we *accept* each new loss, we can never redeem it, or find new life. If not accepted, a negative view will create disgruntled aging.

    1. When we accept and face losses, we'll be able to create a fresh vision for our life. We are no longer afraid to admit to others that we are deprived, wounded, and imperfect in many ways as we grow older. We can share our emotional and spiritual poverty, yet can stand strong and give others the chance to love us to new life. Our *life* is held in our spirit.

        a. Those with positive attitudes toward the maturing process *know* how to welcome back recovering negative thinkers into their ranks. They too have had to admit their fears of aging; they too have had people ho ministered to them; they too have sinned with negative attitudes, but with the help of God and others, they have changed their lives.

III. A necessary aspect of viewing our past is not to stay stuck in it, and to see it as only negative and sinful. It is essential to remember our past so that we can redeem it; but, especially we must remember it so that we know and believe that *we are **survivors**!*

    A. One of the prospects we most fear about our eldering process is that we could become mired in bitterness and resentment and actually end up becoming that sour old person that we've seen others become. This does not have to happen.

        1. Memory can be a graced experience. We just need new lenses through which to see the fresh life taking place within us. We *choose* a positive lens and live what we learn, envision, and create by staying connected to Christ, our Power.

        2. Remembrance will be redemptive if we see the moments of our lives not as past time but *all* as *sacred* time. We then find in the stories of our lives God's action and love always present. This way, our spirit always stays youthful.

        3. Our past, even yesterday as past, can be viewed as a series of failures, tragedies and disappointments. Seen this way, it's easy to become despondent, but we need not make that negative choice. We can always choose Christ-energy.

        4. By staying stuck in the negatives of the past, we could become that which we dread becoming. In contrast to this negative and hopeless view, we recall how Christ dealt with people who felt as we do. We know we are forgiven, and then are able to run to him (as Magdeline did) into endless possibilities.

B. All that we have been and done continues to be a part of us. Our life-history dwells within our being. It is this very dwelling that can give us the new life and wisdom we crave *at this time of life* as we mature into a spiritual-elder-sage.

    1. Outwardly, we are an age that simply tells how many times we have been around the sun. Inwardly, we are every age we have been. All these realities shape our identity and self-understanding. They let us make new discoveries, and see our stuck negative convictions for what they are: destructive.

        a. We may even discover where and from whom we received any negative view of our own aging process. We then can forgive the person(s) and move on to *recreate* an image that is uniquely and positively our own.

    2. Within this remembering and redeeming process, we can substitute a model of wholeness instead of one of perfection. As Ernie Kurtz believes, we can be comfortable with a 'spirituality of imperfection,' and thus grow spiritually.

C. As we share our life-stories, we understand them better. Reminiscing helps to maintain our sense of self, to frame where we went wrong, to see how we can turn our lives around, and to realize how it's OK to need others' love and caring.

    1. This confessing of wrongs gives a sacramental dimension to our lives. It gives us a way to find meaning in our *present* lives by reinterpreting the *past*. We reframe and put back together parts of ourselves that feel lost as we look at the whole picture of our lives, and then plan for the *future*.

    2. Joining the past to the present of our lives becomes a story that supports our identity. It helps us find answers to "Who am I"? "What has my life been all about"? "What is God's overall pattern of my life"?

    3. When we confess to others our stories, we usually come upon something we have known all our lives, but now see it in a brand new way. This in itself is life-giving and it becomes an accepting experience, a resurrection.

        a. Most often, the things we feel we need to confess are the very things that become our greatest assets. *Spiritual eldering is life's greatest educator.*

        b. As we confess, we remember the crises, sift out their meaning and what is life-giving, and allow the rest to fall away; we let go and let God be God. We accept crises as opportunity and as chance to build on the past.

4. When we admit our weakness, we lose our ideal self. This is both frightening and freeing, but the self which emerges has higher, positive spiritual energy.

5. We realize that God has been with us every moment, and all is good. God is within our personal histories; he is part of each chapter of our stories.

6. Our holiness lies in the sacredness of the ordinary. We attend to whatever holiness exits on that holy ground: past, present and future. Our faults never cancel out any of our positive, life-giving actions. Life-giving ones win out!

7. We remember the past, admit wrongdoing, know that we are forgiven, re-image the future, and find clues to where we are going by seeing where we've been. Our sacred stories are unfinished, leaving room for God's action.

We are spiritual elders 'in training,'
in transition unto transformation!

Some Questions to Ponder: Enabling Growth Through Transitions Unto Transformation

1. Have I confessed my negative attitudes toward my eldering process to a trusted friend? How do I feel about sharing my wrongful attitudes? Have I listened to new insights and followed creative suggestions toward developing new attitudes?

2. We have to hear ourselves answer questions at least with our inner ears: "Is my attitude toward eldering what I want for my life? What am I doing to learn about, and plan for, my next transition? What am I doing to become a 'spiritual-elder-sage'?

3. When I look into the mirror, are the lines on my face character lines, smile lines or frown and scowl lines? (Lines don't lie; but they can be re-formed with exercise!)

4. Once my woundedness is accepted, it can be healed and redeemed. How have I accepted this regarding my eldering process? This does not make me less worthy of being loved. Within my 'brokenness' I can be the most beautiful person I can be *now!*

5. When was the last time I made a serious effort to learn more about life-transitions for the next stage of life? If I've not done so, why not? How can I change any indifferent, slide-downhill attitude I may have? This week? This year? How about resources?

6. Do I *make life* happen to me? Or, do I simply let it happen, and remain in negativity?

7. Do I stay stuck in my past life-stages, or am I ready to begin anew to live life forward? Do I help Christ roll back the stone so that a new Resurrection can take place in the next part of my life? (Or, am I content to remain in the tomb where it's safe?)

8. If I refuse to learn about, or to face, personal changes in this transition time of life, I need to admit a major wrong in my life: I'm refusing to 'mature in Christ.' How can I admit this wrong to another person, seek help, and move on with the task of *living!*

9. Do I fear getting older? Which aspect am I anxious about? How can I remember the past, admit of any wrongs when I have refused to be positive about my eldering process, and then move on to re-image my future so that my sacred story continues?

List other questions you have about the eldering process. Use them for further reflections on your journey through transitions unto transformation as you grow into a spiritual-elder-sage.

Some Scripture Quotes:
To Affirm Growth in the Maturing Process

1. "Hence, declare your sins to one another, and pray for one another that you may find healing. The fervent prayer of a holy man is powerful indeed." (Jas 5:16)

2. "Who can forgive sins but God alone." (Mk 2:7)

3. "If your brother should commit some wrong against you, go and point out his fault, but keep it between the two of you. If he listens, you have won your brother over. If he does not listen, summon another, so that every case may stand on he word of two or three witnesses." (Mt 18:15-16)

4. "I came that they might have life, and have it to the full." (Jn 10:10)

5. "The dead man came out bound hand and foot with linen strips, his face wrapped in a cloth. 'Untie him,' Jesus told them, 'and let him go free.' (John 11:44)

6. "Anything you ask me in my name, I will do." (Jn 14:14)

7. "If we acknowledge our sins, he who is just can be trusted to forgive our sins and cleanse us from every wrong." (1 Jn 1:9)

8. "Everyone of us will have to give an account of himself before God. Therefore we must no longer pass judgment on one another. Instead you should resolve to put no stumbling block or hindrance in your brother's way." (Rom 14:12-13)

9. "My brothers, the case may arise among you of someone straying from the truth, and of another bringing him back. Remember: the person who brings a sinner back from his way will save his soul from death and cancel a multitude of sins." (Jas 5:19-20)

10. "Two are better than one: they get a good wage for their labor. If he one falls, the other will lift up his companion. Woe to the solitary man! For if he should fall, he has no one to lift him up." (Ecclesiastes 4:9-10)

11. "Where a lone man may be overcome, two together can resist. A three-ply cord is not easily broken. (Eccl 4:12)

12. "For the Lord gives wisdom...he has counsel in store for the upright, he is the shield of those who walk honestly...protecting the way of his pious ones." (Prv 2:6-8)

13. "If two of you join your voices on earth to pray for anything whatever, it shall be granted you by my Father in heaven. Where two or three are gathered in my name, there am I in their midst." (Mt 18:19-20)

Find some Scripture quotes which speak to your heart at this time of life.

Step 6:Standing Open for Christ's Healing

Were entirely ready to have God remove all these defects of character.

We are ready to stand open to Christ's power daily. We'll ask him to remove any negative attitudes we have toward our maturing process, and ask his help to replace them with an energizing vision and a positive focus.

Promise 6: We will lose interest in selfish things and gain interest in our fellows.

We will rejoice in Christ's healing, and in his help to create a new vision.

****

I. With new openness, we ask Christ to heal any negative attitudes we have toward our eldering process, and to replace them with dynamic, high energy, abundant-life ones.

> **A.** It's only when we are able to admit our character defects and our areas of weakness and vulnerability, that we are entirely ready to have Christ take over.
>
> > **1.** Christ has given us the grace of feeling guilty sometimes, but he gives us another wonderful gift, that of taking away any shame we feel.
> >
> > **2.** St. Paul knew that once he recognized his weakness, he was strong; he then could do all things with Christ who strengthened him. We can do the same.
>
> **B.** In his strength and compassion, Christ offers us courage and insight so that we may look at our negative attitudes, face them, and let him remove them. Our attitude will then change from negative to positive. We're ready for a new mission.
>
> > **1.** Society doesn't want us to face aging. It wants us to hide who we are and to 'be young always.' (Denial!) Getting older is seen almost as a disease!
> >
> > > **a.** Our culture views everything new and young as the epitome of good, and everything old as dispensable, no good, and disposable.
> >
> > **2.** The world tries to get us to buy into its philosophy of false beauty. We need to look deep inside to see if we have bought into this negative attitude that makes older people feel less valued and worthless, simply because of age.
> >
> > > **a.** We need to see if we have been influenced in any way by this attitude. If we have, we ask Christ to remove negative images and to replace them with his higher, positive energy and grace. We open ourselves for his

touch.

b. In owning our own eldering process, we view our physical diminishments and weaknesses more as challenges in our transitions, and less as handicaps. We realize that we don't have to be perfect physically, any more than we do spiritually. We face diminishments, cope, and grow in spirit.

c. Once we accept this fact, we walk tall in the awareness that we are be-coming compassionate toward ourselves and others. This is freeing since we don't have to hide our real self any more; we are loved and worthwhile.

3. We ask Christ to reveal to us where and how we can change any negative, anxious attitudes toward eldering. We look at other older persons, not to criticize, but to decide how *we* want to be as we get older.

4. Others who do not age well, teach us something, too. They hold up to us the truth that there but for the grace of God, I am. They reflect what could be.

5. We give any lack of acceptance of our eldering process to Christ and then see what a difference this makes. By doing so, we can learn from those who have not done this. We'll realize that, except for Christ's grace, we'd be like them.

II. One way we can stand open for Christ's help in replacing our life-less attitude toward eldering with energizing, positive thoughts is by creating our own life-giving Vision-Quest-Commitment statement. This provides Christ-energy for the rest of our lives.

A. *Our Vision*, is what we can yet become; it pulls us toward it like a magnet.

1. We gain a vision of what our potential is from elders and mentors in our lives; we try to live up to that vision by trying to be like those we admire.

a. Our vision of eldering develops from what we have learned, even as small children. As we enter the maturing process, we can formulate our vision, if someone helps us be aware of this and inspires us to formulate our own answer to: *"What kind of spiritual-elder-sage do **I** want to be"?*

2. Our *vision* is comprised of several major elements: physical, mental, emotional, and spiritual. These complement one another in a positive statement.

a. These four elements guide our relationship with God, self, others and world. They guide our choice of new ministry and other aspects of life. They frame how we view our eldering selves: either as spiritual-elder-sages or as people 'over the hill' with nothing more to give, and just getting ready for 'under the hill!' When, in fact, we're now 'on top of the hill.'

3. As we develop our vision, our *will* is the moving force. It helps us to make the right decisions and to stay faithful to the vision, *but it needs help from:*

 a. Awareness, which combines intention and attention.

 b. Specific goal-setting, what we want to accomplish in later years.

 c. A plan of action, some activity which gets the plan on the road.

 d. A lot of 'stick-to-it-tivity,' perseverance when we don't feel like doing it.

 e. Much courage, gumption to complete our plan of action.

 f. Daily quiet time spent with Christ, to form our vision and its expression.

 g. A way to keep the focus, so it is clear and uppermost in our spirit.

B. ***Our Quest***, gives wings to our vision so that we'll fly higher in each transition. It gives a sense of direction, keeps us on track, and sharpens our focus.

 1. The quest part of our resolve is to discover fresh ways of living out our vision in daily life through our positive attitudes during vital transitions.

 2. This quest calls us to formulate our *values*, those behavioral norms of goodness which are lived out through us and govern all we do.

 a. Values put into action are *virtues*. They give a behavior pattern to our life, underpin everything about us, give us our special character, and help channel energies toward the fulfillment of our vision.

 3. Our quest keeps us balanced, open to further maturing, and gives us courage to *change former attitudes or actions*, which stand in the way of our vision.

 4. Our quest is the process of daily hunting, pursuing, searching, and seeking for new ways to refine, and work energetically toward, the pursuit of our Vision.

 5. Our quest takes place in the deepest part of our spirit, keeps our energies on track, and is the methodology which makes our vision do-able.

a. It keeps the balance between what fits our vision and what doesn't.

C. ___Our Commitment___, is a kind of ordination for us to work toward fulfillment of our God-gifted **vision,** discovered for our later years, through the daily **quest** of do-ability.

1. This implies a consecration **by** God and **to** God of our life and ministry; it is a drive, a forward movement toward becoming a unique *spiritual-elder-sage.*

2. This commitment takes all the loyalty and responsibility we can muster. A commitment can be made only to a *person*, not to a cause or an institution. In our case, this requires a fresh commitment to Christ in a brand new way daily.

3. Our commitment becomes a Covenant: a pledge of determination to live the next part of our lives in total Christ-centeredness, at the Spirit's touch, for the Father so that we may be catalysts for positive, loving change in the world.

4. Through our commitment, we'll be more aware that the words the Father said of Christ, "This is my Beloved Son, listen to him," are also said of us: "This is my Beloved One. Listen to _(n)_."

5. This commitment becomes a new consecration to realizing a spiritual depth we never knew before. It includes a fresh look at our life's ministry, at why God created **us**, and propels us to take on new ways of expressing a ministry which voices our bigheartedness, nobility of character, and deep inner quiet.

a. Becoming a spiritual-elder-sage takes courage, a generous dose of God-gifted enthusiasm, and a dynamic Commitment which drives our later years.

III. We put our *Vision-Quest-Commitment* into one ministry statement to be the guiding star of our lives. It gives energy, momentum, purpose, and direction to our eldering..

A. To formulate a 'Vision-Quest-Commitment,' **we need to:**

1. Write down to whom this is pledged--Christ: state which gifts, talents, and values-to-virtues we feel we are being called to use at *this time in life.*

2. Be willing to change: remain flexible as to *how* talents are used in new ways.

3. <u>Use dynamic, energetic verbs:</u> indicate the action we want to take place.

4. <u>State our focus:</u> affirm which group/or for whom we'll give our energies *now*.

B. We *write* our Vision-Quest-Commitment; memories alone are not reliable.

1. This Vision-Quest-Commitment must be clear, with room for growth, thus:

    a. <u>We use the present tense</u> as if it is already being accomplished; *now* is really all we have, and a clear statement of our dream will enliven us.

    b. <u>We phrase it to be applicable</u> to all of life: personal, spiritual, familial, communal, recreational, as well as for ministry, relationships, and leisure.

    c. <u>We use words that are specific</u> but which allow for maturing applications.

2. This *Vision-Quest-Commitment* statement should be no more than one or two sentences long so that it can be remembered, recalled, and put into action easily.

    a. The statement needs to be visible in some manner, framed, as a note in a book, on our mirror, posted on the dashboard, etc.. We need to offer this to Christ daily for his blessing and grace-filled empowerment. The more we do this, the more our life will have purpose and be permeated with gratitude.

Some Questions to Ponder: Enabling Growth Through Transitions Unto Transformation

1. What can you do, practically, to stand before Christ and allow him to remove any negative attitudes you may have toward aging, and replace them with higher energy?

2. If you feel guilty because you've spent too much energy bemoaning getting older, and not enough on creating a new vision of eldering, how can you get rid of the guilt?

3. How can you help to change both church and society's view of older people?

4. Do you believe that you can always be youthful, even if not always young? What do you see as the major difference in the phrases? How can you 'age gracefully'?

5. What are some practical things you can do to remind yourself that you are to walk tall in the realization that **you** are *The Father's Beloved Spiritual-Elder-Sage?*

6. What is your Vision-Quest-Commitment statement for this transition time in life?

7. How can you tap into your higher positive energy at this time of life by slowing your pace, learning to relax, communing with nature, living in the now, trying to see love all around you, and enjoying all of these without feeling guilty? How can you give strength to relational ties, work in moderation, celebrate life, and build fun times into your weekly/daily schedule so these won't get pushed off as lesser needs?

8. What can you do to put creative relaxation into your life, *now*, so you can allow your spiritual eldering to blossom-forth in ways you have not yet even dreamed of?

9. What creative, challenging, energizing, and life-giving opportunities do you see that could open for you as part of your spiritual eldering, *if you wouldn't be afraid to fail?* (A great question to ask yourself is: How old will I be *later* if I undertake this new task *now*? The answer: The same age as if I hadn't taken it; what do I have to lose?)

List other questions you have about the eldering process. Use them for further reflections on your journey through transitions unto transformation as you grow into a spiritual elder-sage.

Some Scripture Quotes:
To Affirm Growth in the Maturing Process

1. "Draw close to God, and he will draw close to you." (Jas 4:8)

2. "Be humbled in the sight of the Lord and he will raise you on high." (Jas 4:10)

3. "For I know well the plans I have in mind for you, says the Lord, plans for your welfare, not for woe, plans to give you a future full of hope." (Jer 29:11)

4. "Do not conform yourselves to this age but be transformed by the renewal of your mind, so that you may judge what is God's will, what is good, pleasing and perfect." (Rom 12:2)

5. "You should now relent and support him so that he may not be crushed by too great a weight of sorrow. I therefore beg you to reaffirm your love for him." (2 Cor 2:7-8)

6. " This treasure we possess in earthen vessels, to make it clear that its surpassing power comes from God and not from us." (2 Cor 4:7)

7. "Continually we carry about in our bodies the dying of Jesus, so that in our bodies the life of Jesus may also be revealed." (2 Cor 4:10)

8. "We do not lose heart, because our inner being is renewed each day even though our body is being destroyed at the same time." (2 Cor 4:16)

9. "We no longer look on anyone is terms of mere human judgment. If at one time we so regarded Christ, we no longer know him by this standard. This means that if any-one is in Christ he is a new creation. The old order has passed away; now all is new! All this has been done by God." (2 Cor 5: 16-18)

10. "You are the temple of the living God." (2 Cor 6:16)

11. "The time came when he who had set me apart before I was born and called me to his favor chose to reveal his Son to me, that I might spread among the Gentiles the good tidings concerning him." (Gal 1:15-16)

12. "Praised be the God and Father of our Lord Jesus Christ, who has bestowed on us in Christ every spiritual blessing in the heavens! God chose us in him before the world began, to be holy and blameless in his sight, to be full of love; he likewise predestined us through Christ Jesus to be his adopted sons--such was his will and pleasure -- that all might praise the glorious favor he has bestowed on us in his beloved." (Eph 1:3-6)

Find some Scripture quotes which speak to your heart at this time of life.

Step 7: Asking Christ's Help to Remove Shortcomings

Humbly ask him to remove our short comings.

We ask Christ daily to remove our shortcomings as we cope with our maturing process, and ask his help in being open to new life and love.

Promise 7: Self-seeking will slip away.

Openness to Christ readies us for the joy of creative, life-giving change.

****

I. In this asking, we experience Christ's help to deal with our frustrations and short-comings during various transitions in our maturing process.

A. Thoughts are forerunners of actions. Positive or negative ones both beget actions. We seek Christ's help creating thoughts which will yield only more love.

1. Risk-taking and transitions are scary, but these must happen in order to have short-comings removed. Loss of the familiar can create beauty and growth.

2. Out of our wounds comes our very healing; Christ appeared after his resurrection with his wound-scars quite visible. So too we have our wound-scars always with us. We are scarred **survivors** as he was, but our scar tissue is stronger and tougher than the original skin; we've changed for the better.

B. Wisdom comes from knowing our scars, living with them, and learning from them. We learn either what *to do* or what *not* to do; this only comes with years.

1. We become spiritual elders only through our wounds and by our attitude toward them. Because we're wounded, we come to realize that we no longer have to be self-righteous over-achievers, or try to do everything ourselves as we minister to others. We no longer have to live a *role*, but only to live and love simply, as human beings who radiate Christ.

a. We no longer have to pray and work at being holy as if this grace depended solely on us. *We are already holy*, therefore we pray and work.

2. As we recognize our scars, we humbly ask Christ to remove our shortcomings (no matter what they are). It takes bighearted honesty and humility to look at our wound-scars, to ask Christ to touch us at our deepest center, and to heal whatever he finds there that needs his healing touch, even if these are unknown to us.

3. Too often, we are wounded because we equate a life surrendered to Christ, and to the living of his Gospel, with a kind of subservience to institutional Church. The two are not the same: we do not need to surrender our life to institutional Church in order to serve Christ, but we *do* need to surrender to Christ in order to serve his people through an institutional Church.

    a. Commitment can never be made to an institution; it must be made to a person, one we love deeply enough to give our life to: Christ.

    b. One of our *shortcomings* is to confuse the two concepts. We are *not* our role; as we mature, we realize in new ways that we are much more than our role. We are Christ-centered men and women of the Gospel.

    c. The longevity factor alone has called our attention to this and calls for major change. Many, however, have given their lives to Church, instead of to Christ and have difficulty living apart from a Church-assumed role.

    d. By 'living Church' instead of 'living Christ' maturing is stifled. We feel we must fit into a certain box of expectations. This is a serious wrong which needs forgiving and a fault that needs correcting as we mature.

    e. Role-boundaries which have our welfare in mind are one thing; role-boundaries which inhibit human and spiritual growth and hem us in are quite another. Part of our becoming a spiritual elder is to differentiate between the two and to act accordingly, so that we will mature in Christ.

II. Our shortcomings involve our whole person, as does our integrity; a person with integrity is single hearted and keeps life going in the right direction: *toward Christ*.

    A. In Step Six, we asked Christ to remove our defects of character, our negative views our eldering process. We now realize that our struggles to change this view will fail unless *we ready ourselves for this change* and have patience.

        1. When we are ready to change, it's amazing to find how much help is available. We only have to be open, to look for it, and to surrender to Christ's power in us.

    B. The shortcomings of refusing to plan for our transitions in our eldering process include those which close us to further growth on physical, mental, moral, and spiritual levels We must plan in all these areas; they *all* need <u>work</u>.

        1. Six things are absolutely necessary to have abundant life; *we **must***:

a. <u>Maintain a proper, balanced diet</u>: portion control/calorie restriction are best. Vitamins, meds and adequate rest are also essential to support diet.

b. <u>Exercise</u>: daily for at least 20 minutes. It doesn't need to be strenuous. Deep breathing is important. Tai Chi, Yoga, Pilates, and slow walks work.

c. <u>Socialize</u>: have friends, have fun, take time off away from ordinary routine. Take the initiative to phone, write, etc.; we do it our own way.

d. <u>Do fun things *just to have fun*</u>: do relaxing activities; create time simply to enjoy life. Build these activities into each day. Let our inner-child *play.*

e. <u>Learn something new daily:</u> read, study a foreign language, have a hobby; do crosswords; watch educational TV. Learning must be *lifelong.*

f. <u>Deepen our prayerlife</u>: try new prayerforms; break out of old have-to forms and create more want-to ways to build friendship with Christ which are different from previous years. There's no best way, except to *grow!*

C. Staying stuck in the same old ways is a shortcoming. It's safe, in a way, but we need to cross-over to a more mature eldering. *Transitions* means *change;* so *we'll:*

1. <u>Safeguard independence</u> and a sense of autonomy in order to function as vitally and joyfully as possible; we'll get help, if needed, but not give up!

2. <u>View wrinkles as badges of courage</u> and gray hair as a mark of distinction.

3. <u>Be a loving parent-image</u> to each young person we meet, even incidentally.
4. <u>Find a way</u> to pass on gently the wisdom of our years to younger persons.

5. <u>Engage</u> in some art, music or language classes to stimulate the right-brain.

6. <u>Pass on</u> some of the skills we have to at least one younger person.

7. <u>Get into volunteering</u>, especially to those who need our special talent/skill.

8. <u>Work to change the image</u> of eldering from one of merely *dependency* to that of a Spiritual-Elder-Sage in society, the media and the church.

9. <u>Let our voice be heard</u> regarding anything that has to do with eldering so that public attitudes and laws will change. (AARP is one way.)

10. <u>Remain open-minded</u> to see where others can still teach us something.

11. Keep our curiosity alive and experiment; we'll do things we never did before.

12. Open our imagination to do something creative, though no one may notice.

13. Keep our sense of humor and not take criticisms seriously or personally.

14. Be open to develop our love-life, and to loving and being loved in new ways.

15. Greet each new day with gratitude as God's love-gift to us, and then share it.

D. The major shortcoming--lack of preparation for our necessary transitions-- inhibits our growth in becoming a spiritual-elder-sage; *anticipation* and *planning* are vital.

1. Prevention, treatment and cure of ailments/sickness are part of this awareness; they are associated with, but not intrinsic to, growing older. They are part of all life and need to be acknowledged, worked at, and accepted or adapted to, for positive eldering. We will no longer expect doctors and pills alone to 'cure us'; we must take better control of our own wellness process in any way we can.

2. The quality of healthy years, made possible throughout our extended lifespan, is drastically improved for all of us. However, these improvements must be planned for by persons thirty and over if they are to be energetic, spiritual elders.

    a. Becoming crippled, disabled, 'stupid,' and doddering in a nursing home is ***not*** the inevitable fate of maturing. Our eldering years can be the best years of our life because of our lived wisdom, *if* we are open to prepare and plan for these transition years, on our journey unto transformation.

3. Long before we're thought to be old, we must begin to craft our own eldering by dreaming how we want to be as a spiritual elder. Shortcomings will lessen.

    a. If we dream it, we can become it. We imagine self at 80, 90 or 100. Then, we work toward becoming this ideal elder by framing values, viewing talents to be developed, and honing dimensions of our temperament and personality to fit our image. We visit this ideal often to be encouraged.

b. <u>We ask</u>: "How ought I plan my retirement? What life-style should I choose? How can I grow intellectually, spiritually? Where should I live?"

c. <u>We never let diminishment touch our spirit</u>. It is as young as when God first created it; we can't stay young always, but our spirit can stay youthful.

d. <u>We work to become joyful spiritual elders</u>. Persons who are crotchety when they are older were that way earlier in life and just became *fixat*ed.

e. <u>Spiritual elders are respected and learned from</u>. They are wisdom-keepers and provide security, spirituality, anchoring, mentoring and a sense of belonging to the next generation. *'Families first'* should be our motto, **not** 'children first.' *Healthy families with spiritual elders form healthy children.*

f. <u>We ask</u>: "What gifts do I *now have* that can help make the world a better place in which to live? How best can I use these? Where? With whom"?

g. <u>We grow.</u> Through the transitions of our eldering, we grow in friendship with God from being: *a child*, one cared for by God, to *a disciple*, one who follows what God wants, to *being a steward*, one who then takes God's message, and, *with Christ,* adds personal touches, and passes it on.

Some Questions to Ponder:
Enabling Growth Through Transitions Unto
Transformation

1. In asking Christ to remove our shortcomings, most of us have fears: (a) that we'll be too afraid to do what we need to in order to change, and so may remain stuck with old negative views of growing older; and (b), that we will change, and may not like the new person we are becoming. Do you subscribe to one of these fears? Why?

2. List two or three specific shortcomings in your maturing process that you want removed; then list how you can do something to help bring this removal about.

3. What will be the benefit to yourself and to others when these shortcomings are removed? How would you feel about the new growth you experience?

4. Have you seen growth in any area of your eldering process? Where? How?

5. Christ is willing to remove your shortcomings, especially as they relate to this new transition time of life; he will empower you to change a little each day. How can this *new you* just waiting to be freed, be realized? Today? This week? This year?

6. There's a lot of spiritual power contained in asking Christ to remove our shortcomings because of the word *humbly*. St. Teresa said that humility is truth, but self-knowledge is only the beginning of wisdom and inner growth. It's what we *do* with this wisdom that is more important. The question now is, "How can you live Christ in the world today, *at the age you now are"?*

7. Without the enabling power of Christ's presence within you, you will not be able to eliminate obstacles which interfere with the fullness of life he gives. What can you do to help Christ accomplish his purpose in you? Today? This week? This year?

8. Christ will answer your request to remove shortcomings when you dispose yourself for his grace-filled touch of empowerment. How have you disposed yourself for creative, positive eldering through natural means? Reading? Prayer? Friends? Study?

9. On your way to becoming a spiritual elder, all you need do is to decide to live up to the abundant life with which Christ fills you. What can you do to be aware of this?

List other questions you have about the eldering process. Use them for further reflections on your journey through transitions unto transformation as you grow into a spiritual-elder-sage.

Some Scripture Quotes:
To Affirm Growth in the Maturing Process

1. "Yes, God so loved the world that he gave his only son that whoever believes in him may not die but may have eternal life." (Jn 3:16)

2. "Scripture says, ' No one who believes in him will be put to shame.'" (Rom 10:11)

3. "Whoever drinks the water I give will never be thirsty; no, the water I give shall become a fountain within him, leaping up to provide eternal life." (Jn 4:14)

4. "Trust in the Lord with all your heart, on your own intelligence rely not; in all your ways be mindful of him and he will make straight your paths." (Prv 3:5-6)

5. "All this I tell you that my joy may be yours and your joy may be complete." (Jn 15:11)

6. "Sing to the Lord, you his faithful ones, and give thanks to his holy name." (Ps 30:5)

7. "Dismiss all anxiety from your minds. Present your needs to God in every form of prayer and in petitions full of gratitude." (Phil 4:6)

8. "But if we acknowledge our sins, he who is just can be trusted to forgive our sins and cleanse us from every wrong. " (1 Jn 1:9)

9. "For these I pray--not for the world but for those you have given me, for they are really yours." (Jn 17:9)

10. "A lamp to me feet is your word, a light to me path." (Ps 119:105)

11. "Take delight in the Lord and he will grant you your heart's requests." (Ps 37:4)

12. "Whoever believes in the son has life eternal." (Jn 3:36a)

Find some Scripture quotes which speak
to your heart at this time of life.

Step 8: Remembering Hurts to Effect Healing

Made a list of all persons we had harmed,
and became willing to make amends to them all.

*We become aware of those in our life whom we have harmed by
communicating a negative view of aging, and make amends.*

<u>Promise 8:</u> Our whole attitude and outlook upon life will change.

*We'll communicate a positive attitude toward the aging process; our
outlook on this time of life will change into a more upbeat one.*

****

I. Oftentimes, in our maturing process, we hurt people simply because we are going through the aging process. We have a hard time differentiating between our *needs* and *wants*. We then put undue demands upon others because of this confusion.

    A. When overwhelmed with the incorrect balance of these two powerful forces, we need to back off, think it through, and learn to differentiate between them.

        1. We need to apologize for any unnecessary requests and/or demands we've put upon others using age as an excuse, or because we 'deserved' extra attention.

        2. Once this awareness is established, we will be able to make amends sooner, and will have fewer reasons to create undue demands/requests in the future.

    B. In our growth toward becoming a spiritual elder, a positive, creative attitude is vital or we'll not be able to nurture our own, or another's, spiritual vitality. Without a positive view of aging, we impart negative emotions and attitudes.

        1. Sometimes we know whom we have harmed by our negativity, but are not willing to let go of pessimistic feelings. A blessing sent to them daily helps.

        2. The *will* to make amends does not rest with feelings, it rests with choice. It requires that we recognize where we have communicated negative views of aging. Then we can be willing to apologize, and live more positive messages.

        3. We need to own the inconsiderate things we are doing, or have done, because of negative attitudes. These have harmed others, and it will be difficult to take responsibility for them. Yet, when we start making sincere apologies and try to make amends, we're on the healing path to becoming a spiritual-elder-sage.

C. In making amends, we strive for a peaceful relationship with *Christ*, *self*, *others*, and *world*. The peacefulness of our eldering process can be disrupted by an imbalance in any of these areas. By choosing higher, positive energy, we succeed.

    1. Persons who strive for balance in these areas are those who mature with an inner peace that shows. They'll *not* become grouchy or negative as they age.

    2. The other person's response to our offerings of amends is not as important as the courage we've shown to make them, and the freedom we feel thereafter.

II. Some of the ways we have harmed or hurt others are obvious; many are not. Another's negativity affects us; ours affects theirs, to a greater or lesser degree.

    A. Impatience often becomes a harmful fault as one grows into the later years. Many people say: "I can't help it. I can't change. I'm too old. I've always been that way."

        1. There's a lot to be said about counting to ten before responding when things don't go according to our *wants*. Slamming things, raising one's voice, jerking objects away from another, throwing things, and vulgar language are common expressions of not being at peace with God, self, others, and world.

            a. Reversing the above listed actions are the first steps in making amends to another who was within our environment when we expected perfection, but didn't get it. Older persons *can* change, if they *want* to. This is the time when eldering people must turn to the wisdom gained over the years.

            b. A simple verbal, "I'm sorry," will do wonders to help clear the air. It will help us realize that this small gesture will keep us from becoming unpleasant, disgruntled, grouchy older persons who aren't perfect either.

    B. To blame our impatience on getting older is a simply a lame excuse and is not helpful to anyone. We need to look at how we have contributed to the problem by expecting everything to go as *we* would like, at all times and everywhere.

        1. Somehow, blaming impatience on aging, seems to give us permission to behave this way. We can't help getting older, so we consider it a handicap which gives us the right and freedom to do what *we* want, and to expect that everyone around us understands this and lets us get away with this attitude.

        2. During the transitions of life, we withdraw just what we put in, so we had better deposit lots of positive thoughts, attitudes and memories long before we have to begin drawing them out of our eldering bank account.

III. Our responsibility to make amends is the logical extension of the Two Great Commandments; we need to *make amends to ourselves* as well as to others.

A. As we get older, we realize that we have many spiritual energies which have been covered up, or not acknowledged, simply because we have concentrated too much on ridding ourselves of faults instead of concentrating on being a ***survivor.***

1. Much of life's energies have been taken up with staying away from some kind of harmful behavior. In our transition time, as we make amends, we shift this focus. If not, we'll die with the song God gave us still unsung in our hearts.

B. As part of maturing into a spiritual elder, we must change negative views and make amends to the deepest part of ourselves, our spirit. Then, creative energies which have been stifled for years, will be released to give life and love to others.

1. As we make these amends to ourselves, we allow Christ's dynamic energy to take over our spirit more and more so that we'll communicate positive energy. When we do this, ***we are:***

a. <u>More in touch</u> with our life's purpose and meaning.

b. <u>More enabled</u> to have both the discernment and the courage to do what we know is the highest good, and the truest expression of our love and life.

c. <u>Enabled to feel the energy</u> of transmitting life, love and light to others.

d. <u>Empowered to grow</u> in the wisdom of our years, and to face limitations as well as our untapped potential for fresh growth and vitality.

e. <u>Enabled to carry out our decisions</u> which are geared to giving life, love, light, and spiritual energy to anyone to whom we want to give this gift.

f. <u>Called to have a new kind of compassion</u> for ourselves and for others, as we look for different ways to be of service; new life equals new service.

g. <u>Open to listen to the inner movements of our spirit;</u> we have faced our failures and fears; we are now ready to believe in our deepest self and to trust our essential goodness and Christ like radiance shining from within.

h. <u>Enabled and empowered</u> to create the life we really want, to live the life we have left in fulfilling, creative, and positive ways. (Perhaps to 120!)

    i. <u>Challenged by Christ</u> to create a zest for life that reaches to the core of our very beings, so that the new life, light, and love he has placed within us as *his gift to us in our maturing years* are freed for eternal possibilities.

IV. In our eldering, as we make amends, also to ourselves, Christ releases in us the new kinds of spiritual energies we need in order to live a full, vibrant, more spiritual life.

    A. Though these energies were in us before, we needed both our past mistakes and the gleaned wisdom of our maturing years to recognize these gifts and to pursue them.

        1. Christ told us that if we love ourselves, we will love others. So, as we make amends to ourselves, we make amends to others also, as least indirectly. Some of the *spiritual energies,* important and integral to a spiritual elder's vision <u>are</u>:

            a. <u>A renewed self-awareness and self-affirmation</u>, which helps us to know and affirm the truth of who we are: the Beloved son/daughter of the Father.

            b. <u>A belief that we are meant to be bearers and transmitters of life in *all*</u> <u>the transitions of our life</u>, which helps us to change the *way* we bear and give it.

            c. <u>A lived wisdom</u>, which gives us a keener discernment, and discrimination.

            d. <u>A deeper sense of compassion</u>, which is the ability to 'suffer with another.' We no longer pity them; pity does nothing to alleviate pain, compassion does.

            e. <u>A stronger sense of courage</u> which releases a related energy of forgiveness. It allows us to be willing to change what we can, to accept what we cannot change, and gives us higher energy to move on with the job of *living **love.***

            f. <u>A renewed sense of commitment to our life's vision</u> which enables us to make fresh life-choices, to carry them out, and not to waver.

            g. <u>A deepened sense that we are healers</u> which helps us to see the universe more clearly from God's viewpoint--as united and as one. Grace within is released to heal, at all levels, our relationship with God, self, others and world.

h. <u>A dynamic friendship with Christ</u> which takes us into this vibrant way of being. We concentrate not so much on how much we love Christ, but on how he first loves us and is traveling this road with us, always present, always near.

B. Our ability to make amends is an important aspect of the spiritual energy of courage. Initially, we apologize if possible. Later, we may do something to resume or to heal the relationship, *if only by sending the other(s) a blessing daily.*

1. We may decide that the relationship is toxic, not important, or is impossible to resume. We no longer work at it, but healing happens through our blessing.

C. We can make amends to those we've harmed without face-to-face contact even if they are no longer physically accessible (death, distance, refusal to meet), if there is or would be a rejection of an apology, if communication would not promote reconciliation, or if an attempt could or would cause harm to self or others.

1. In prayer, we ask Christ to heal all of us. Each day we send a blessing to anyone we have harmed and to those who have harmed us. Healing will happen.

2. In our eldering, many of our friends and family are out of our life for one reason or another. Yet, making amends in some way is *essential* to our becoming spiritual elders, if we are to grow in wisdom, age and grace before God and others. Even if God and we are the only ones who witness this amend-making, healing will take place within us, and negative energy will not be passed-on to future generations. It will stop with us.

Some Questions to Ponder:
Enabling Growth Through Transitions
UntoTransformation

1. In what ways have you harmed others by a self-pitying attitude toward your own aging process? What are your favorite self-put-downs regarding this transition?

2. Can you list some human limitations that come with eldering which contribute to a sense of impatience with yourself, and which you take out on others?

3. Are you timid about apologizing to another because of harming them? Why?

4. Why do you think that someone would not want to forgive you?

5. Why is asking for forgiveness so hard to do?

6. Is there anyone you have harmed who is no longer in your life? How so you plan to make amends? A letter? An undelivered letter? A blessing sent to them?

7. How do you plan to send a daily blessing to those you have harmed in any way?

8. How do you plan to make amends to yourself for harming *you*? Plan for more leisure, without feeling guilty? Taking on a more healthy lifestyle? Exercising?

9. In this eldering time of life, how can you shift the focus of your life's energies away from harming others (breaking relationship with them), to the positive energy of releasing more of your love for them, if only by sending them a blessing?

10. In making amends, do you believe you are a healer *of* and *in* the world?
    How does this free you for both sending and being a blessing for others?

11. How do you see yourself as being a healer? How do *you* express this?
    How have you stopped communicating to others a negative view of your eldering?

List other questions you have about the eldering process. Use them for further reflections on your journey through transitions unto transformation as you grow into a spiritual-elder-sage.

Some Scripture Quotes:
To Affirm Growth in the Maturing Process

1. "Do to others what you would have them do to you." (Lk 6:31)

2. "Why look at the speck in your brother's eye when you miss the plank in your own. How can you say to your brother, ' Let me take that speck out of your eye.' while all the time the plank remains in your own? You hypocrite! Remove the plank from your own eye first; then you will see clearly to take the speck from your brother's eye." (Mt 7:3-5)

3. "Then Peter came up and asked him, 'Lord, when my brother wrongs me, how often must I forgive him? Seven times?' 'No,' Jesus replied, 'not seven times; I say, seventy times seven times.' " (Mt 18:21-22)

4. "Sanctify yourselves, then, and be holy; for I, the Lord, your God am holy. Be careful, therefore, to observe what I, the Lord, who make you holy, have prescribed." (Lv 20:7-8)

5. "If you bring your gift to the altar and there recall that your brother has anything against you, leave your gift at the altar, go first to be reconciled with your brother, and then come and offer your gift." (Mt 5:23-24)

6. "Give us today our daily bread, and forgive us the wrong we have done as we forgive those who wrong us." (Mt 6:11-12)

7. " If you forgive the faults of others, your heavenly Father will forgive you yours. If you do not forgive others, neither will your Father forgive you." (Mt 14-15)

8. "You have heard the commandment, 'You shall love your countryman but hate your enemy.' My command to you is: love your enemies, pray for your persecutors." (Mt 5:43-44)

9. "The Lord is my shepherd; I shall not want. In verdant pastures he gives me repose; beside restful waters he leads me; he refreshes my soul. He guides me in right paths for his name's sake." (Ps 23:2-3)

Find some Scripture quotes which speak
to your heart at this time of life.

Step 9: Making Amends Where Possible

Made direct amends to such people wherever possible,
except when to do so would injure them or others.

*We become aware of the changes taking place within us during our eldering process;
we affirm them, and, when feasible, make amends to those against whom we have
acted inappropriately when we used 'aging' as an excuse.*

Promise 9: Fear of people and of economic insecurity will leave us.

Fear of getting older will leave us; we'll no longer treat self or others as old.

****

I. Our spirituality is our response to God's "I love you;" it touches every aspect of our lives and enables us to have a creative, positive attitude in all we do.

    A. It empowers us with openness and a willingness to change. This way, we do not stay mired in our old ways. We gently go through life's transitions, on our way to becoming elegant spiritual elders, as persons who have 'lots of love to give yet.'

        1. As we come to understand changes taking place within us, we'll allow Christ's compassion to take over our spirituality. We'll not strike out or use self-pity as ways of coping with the eldering process. We choose love as our coping mechanism, and will be better able to make amends where and when feasible.

        2. Once we have *accepted* our eldering process as life's greatest educator, we will better be able to manage this growth-filled time without impatience or self-pity. With the wisdom of years, we will be gentle with ourselves and with others who are on the same road through transitions unto transformation.

        3. As we plan and grow in our eldering, we'll realize that we have nothing to lose, but everything to gain if we focus on living our new years with love and a greater inner peace and tranquility. Making amends to others and to ourselves becomes a way of life as we *choose* to live in positive, higher energy.

    B. The social environment of negativity affects everyone in that space, just as second-hand smoke does when it infiltrates and pollutes another's lungs.

        1. As we get older, we realize that there is no such thing as a wrong that hurts no one but self. If we hurt ourselves, there is always a ripple effect because of the self-hatred and feelings of worthlessness involved.

2. When we choose love, the environment created spreads out to affect every-thing our life touches. When we strike out, even in lesser matters, we change the environment from a positive, higher, spiritual, life-giving energy field to a lower, negative energy field. This causes relational disruptions.

II. One of the major tasks of becoming a spiritual elder is to be a healer of the world-- our own, and the larger world around us. As we positively cope with life's losses, we are able better to make amends and to tap into higher energy without injuring others.

A. In our brokenness, we've often not been lovingly present to others in a Christ-like way. We have focused too much on our imperfections and losses, instead of on our positive, grace-filled potential. Actually, if faced, *losses lead to new life!*

B. A major reason we strike out against others is because we are suffering many *losses* from people and events which have been securities for us in the past. By not affirming these losses, we cannot cope with them. Therefore, we scapegoat these feelings of loss onto others and act inappropriately toward them.

1. By affirming and dealing with *losses,* we are able to make amends for any scapegoating. This forgiveness frees our spirit from the harmful cycle of hurt. In the wisdom of years, we realize more keenly that we need to *face and deal with our losses*, and then we are less likely to act inappropriately to others.

2. To help cope with losses, we make up our minds never to treat ourselves as old, or to treat any other person as old either, no matter what age they are. We may be handicapped at bit, but never old, which means we've given up.

C. We grieve losses daily, even though we may not be aware of it. Some regard every ache and pain, every physical diminishment and discomfort as an outrage, assault, or humiliation. There are others who cope by choosing to dwell on what can yet *be done*, rather than waste creative energy on what they can no longer do.

1. The French writer, Paul Claudel, says: " Eighty years old: no eyes left, no ears, no teeth, no legs, no wind! And when all is said and done, how astonishingly well one does without them!"

2. According to the social scientist, Robert Peck, the major difference between the two is the difference between *body preoccupation*, and *body transcendence*. The first views physical aging as both our enemy and master; the second views aging as a unique, creative time of life and makes peace with it.

a. In dealing with life's losses in our spiritual eldering, we can see ourselves as half-dead, and incapable of anything. Or, more healthily, we see ourselves as persons who perceive losses, but still will concentrate on what can yet be done in spite of the losses and, maybe even, *because* of them.

    b. People cannot make us feel any certain way over our losses, e.g. mad. Our makeup and character dictate how we react to feelings of loss, and to how we make amends for inappropriate responses to these emotions.

III. In dealing with losses, we cannot rush the process. When it's time to accept them, we will know. This dealing is a process, not an event, and takes time. The healing will take place a layer at a time, as with any injury. As we heal, we are moving on.

    A. In the process of not accepting losses, or in not knowing how to accept them, we may have acted inappropriately. However, if our actions were not meant to harm, but others read something into them, this is beyond our control. Amends are best made then by praying for them, and by surrendering everything to Christ for healing.

        1. We may never carry hurt, pain and unforgiveness to our graves. As an essential part of eldering, we do our best and then give Christ the rest for healing.

    B. It's not always possible to go back and make amends. Death, separation or lack of openness on the part of the other may stand in the way. Our *attitude and willingness* to make amends is the key here, even if this never takes place. When making amends is not possible, we can substitute a kindness to an unrelated person as our gesture of willingness to spread love and positive energy, and healing takes place.

    C. Carrying hurts around is like carrying a sack of old garbage; it continues to firment even as we drag it. Soon we can't tell the banana peel from the apple core. Our perception is warped simply from the age of it all; mere memory distorts.

        1. If we've not given the 'garbage' to Christ to be changed into to fertilizer for the garden of our eldering years, now is the time to do so. If not, there'll be no flowers or seeds; we'll just have smelly garbage to carry which will only serve to repel others. We'll then wonder why we're alone in our older years!

IV. As we face, deal with, grieve and mourn our losses, we also need to make amends to ourselves, whom we have often harmed more than we have harmed others. This is a difficult process, but one full of grace in our later years.

A. *Grief* is the feeling of pain we have over losses; ***mourning*** is the way we express and handle the grief. If we have been harsh, unforgiving, and overly critical of ourselves as we elder, and have not done our homework in the loss area, we'll treat others the same as we treat ourselves. If we *do* our homework, we'll be more spontaneous and ready to make amends for harsh behavior; negativity will halt.

1. Physical changes often have negative effects on us, if we buy into society's image of beauty, with all the tucking that takes place. Instead, we see that we can be attractive at *any age* just by helping Mother Nature in the ordinary simple ways of diet, exercise, health care, rest, grooming, etc..

   a. By helping ourselves to be the best we can be at the age we are, we are able to forgive our bodies for aging, and to forgive ourselves for thinking that we must always look as we did in years past, or like someone else!

2. Body-image is enhanced by acceptance of the fact that our spirit shows. No matter how our body changes, our spirit never ages, it becomes stronger.

   a. As we become spiritual elders, we take good care of our bodies so that our spirit may shine out even more radiantly and create a quiet peace all around us that speaks of an ever-deepening friendship with Christ.

   b. When we affirm our own inner beauty, we are giving the world a message it needs: true beauty is more than skin deep. It's only a wise spiritual elder who has worked on the inner life, who can carry the message of spiritual youthfulness to our society, which needs this concept.

3. We remember that everyone makes mistakes. To dwell on them only prevents us from tapping into the higher energy of our spirit where Christ's loving presence fills us with his love, light and new life. In him, we are survivors!

   a. When we keep on playing the tapes of our mistakes, faults, or even sins, we are saying to Christ that we really don't trust that he forgave us. He said that he came for sinners; all he wants is our open, loving heart.

   b. Not to forgive ourselves is as if we are kneeling before Christ, saying over and over that we're sorry, when all he really wants to do is to say to us: "Come close, that's all in the past. Don't let it ruin our present precious moment together *now*; just let me love you." Then, he pours precious oil on our heads and rubs it in until it flows down, all over us, with his love!

B. By facing and accepting our losses, we have greater compassion for ourselves and so for others in their losses. We make amends to ourselves by granting to ourselves those seventy times seven chances we try to give to others.

1. We are what our thoughts are, and we pay attention to these, for they are forerunners of our acts. As we face losses, and live and give compassion, amends will be made through our daily positive attitudes and actions. We'll be dwelling on gains from the losses, rather than on the losses themselves. As we focus on being survivors, making amends becomes so much easier!

C. The more we handle our losses as gains, the fewer amends we will have to make, because we will be creating an environment of peace around us. Losses become gains for greater inner growth as we become spiritual elders.

D. Many people have found life's most creative gains within losses: <u>Beethoven</u>, deaf and near ninety, created his *Fifth*; at ninety-nine, <u>George Burns</u>, was still entertaining; <u>Edmund Hoyle</u>, at seventy-six, wrote "according to Holye;" <u>Mother Theresa</u>, very active at eighty-five; <u>Clara Barton</u>, became President of the Red Cross at eighty three; <u>Michaelangelo</u>, still painting at eighty-six; <u>Frank L.Wright</u>, designed the Guggenheim Museum at ninety-one; <u>Mae West</u>, still acting at eighty-five!

1. *Talk about turning losses to gains!* What mentors are these, and many more too numerous to mention here. What amends did they have to make in order to get as far as they did. We have much to learn from them, and others like them. They didn't let getting older become an excuse for not focusing on the gains from their losses.

Some Questions to Ponder:
Enabling Growth Through Transitions Unto Transformation

1. For you, what is the easiest situation in which to make amends? What are some ways that work for you? What fits your personality, temperament and spirituality?

2. In your eldering process, how can you now handle making amends in ways that you would not have done earlier in life because of your present lived-wisdom?

3. As you get older, how do the hurts of the past still affect your present life? How do you look at those whom you have harmed? At those who have harmed you?

4. What was the most difficult situation for you to make amends? How did you do?

5. How do you make amends to yourself? How do you feel when you do this? How does making amends to yourself affect your making amends to others?

6. What are some of the losses you are experiencing in your eldering process? How do you handle these? What are your feelings of grief? How do you mourn the losses of eldering in a positive manner so that your focus stays on the gains in the losses?

7. What are some obvious losses of eldering? Some non-obvious ones? Some inevitable ones? What do these losses feel like to you? How do you react to them?

8. How can you live as a *survivor* in the very loss-gain cycle, and make amends?

9. How can you be more gentle with yourself, so as to let this gentleness rub off on to others with compassion? Do you ever pamper yourself as you experience losses so that you can get through them better? How? What works for you?

10. Facing life's losses, grieving and mourning them, healing from the losses, making amends for inappropriate behavior, and being a survivor are interrelated. How do you see the relationship? How does this help you to celebrate the fact that you truly are a survivor as a creative, positive spiritual-elder-sage?

List other questions you have about the eldering process. Use them for further reflections on your journey through transitions unto transformation as you grow into a spiritual-elder-sage.

Some Scripture Quotes:
To Affirm Growth in the Maturing Process

1. "Give and it shall be given to you. Good measure pressed down, shaken together, running over, will they pour into the fold of your garment. For the measure you measure with will be measured back to you." (Lk 6:38)

2. "Stop worrying." (Lk 12:29)

3. "Man of God that you are,...seek after integrity, piety, faith, love steadfastness, and a gentle spirit." (1 Tm 6:11)

4. "Go first to be reconciled with your brother, and them come and offer your gift." (Mt 5:24)

5. "Jesus saw their faith, he said to the paralyzed man, 'My son, your sins are forgiven... I command you: Stand up! Pick up your mat and go home.' " (Mk 2:5,11)

6. "The eye is the lamp of your body. When your eyesight is sound, your whole body is lighted up, but when your eyesight is bad, your body is in darkness. Take care, then, that your light is not darkness. If your whole body is lighted up and not partly in darkness, it will be as fully illuminated as when a lamp shines brightly for you." (Lk 11:34-36)

7. "You shall love the Lord your God with all your heart, with all your soul, with all your strength, and with all your mind; and your neighbor as yourself." (Lk 10:27)

8. "Love your enemies, pray for your persecutors." (Mt 5:44)

9. "Come to me, all you who are weary and find life burdensome, and I will refresh you. Take my yoke upon your shoulders and learn from me, for I am gentle and humble of heart. Your souls will find rest, for my yoke is easy and my burden light." (Mt 11:28-30)

Find some Scripture quotes which speak to your heart at this time of life.

Step 10: Continuing Personal Inventory

Continued to take personal inventory and
when we were wrong promptly admitted it.

*We stand open to Christ, and inventory our growth into spiritual eldering.
We reflect on how we have loved, and where or when we've not loved. We ask Christ to
help us admit our wrongs, and for his help to give love now.*

Promise 10: We'll intuitively know how to handle situations which used to baffle us.

We'll know a new depth of wisdom as we pray for healing and radiate love.

****

I. As we get older, remembering as an inventory is vital. It acts as a life-review, helps us to reframe our lives, find new meaning, and relive parts of our lives that we never let ourselves feel or think about. Because of our training or upbringing, because we were too afraid or timid to think for ourselves, or because we were not aware of the influence certain events had on our life, we may not have reflected sufficiently on their lasting impact.

    A. In doing this inventory, we need to look at our family of origin, the one where we grew up. This is the single greatest factor in our lives which influences everything we do; we can adapt and change things learned there, but we can never not be a part of it.

        1. As a vital part of becoming a spiritual-elder-sage, we must take our life's inventory. We need to walk back through our family of origin, rename our hurts, our unmet needs, and our repressed emotions. We must also identify graces and blessings, and acknowledge where we, and it, went *right* as well as wrong.

            a. In doing this, we become "smart from the heart" (12-Steps). There is no such unit as a perfect family, nor a totally imperfect one; each is on a journey to perfect love. Looking back helps us to learn and heal, *not* to blame.

            b. As we grew, we were told to be or do things because that was the only way our parents knew, who learned from their parents, who learned from theirs, etc.. They tried to do their best, just as we try to do our best.

            c. To do the blame-game regarding parents and family for who we are today, is not to take responsibility for our own growth and spirituality.

2. Taking an inventory-review of our life is essential to being a spiritual elder. In it, we can see what we did right, as well as where our human weakness caused us to make wrong decisions. By facing these two aspects of life, we can move on to higher spiritual energy and creative love in the next transition of life.

3. As we do the inventory, we admit the bright and the dark in our lives and in our family of origin; these factors influenced our growth, development, and spirituality.

B. In the wisdom of our eldering, writing our autobiography is of great importance as we do an inventory. This helps us to gain perspective on our life's story, and to find, clarify and deepen the meaning of the accumulated experiences of our life.

    1. This process will help us to set fresh goals. It'll help us to see where our lives have mattered and help us to find a new sense of purpose. It will enhance feelings of worthwhileness, and will help promote successful adaptation to our eldering. It will assist us in making positive, creative choices for each budding transition.

        a. An inventory-autobiography helps us to see where we went wrong, but also to know what we did right. Through it, we grasp the wholeness of our life, which is a positive contribution to well-being in later life.

        b. By writing our story, we also write our family story. In the inventory-writing, we will also be creating an important legacy to be handed on to the seventh generation, one we'll not see. (A Native American custom.)

    2. This writing evokes reminiscences. The recall of past events helps direct us to examine these memories from the lived perspective of our present life. This life review helps us to script our lives and our role in family as we inventory our:

    a. Major growth-points of life.

    b. Family, with its dark and light sides.

    c. Career, jobs and ministry choices, now and during our past years.

    d. View of money and its place throughout our lifetime.

    e. Health, all that relates to well-being, and how we have handled sickness throughout our life. (Positively or negatively?)

    f. Body image, especially acceptance of our bodies as we get older.

g. Sexual identity, roles, fears and experiences.

h. Life's goals, and all that keeps us connected to Christ, the Source of our life's energy, as we continue to create a life-giving, love-giving purpose for daily living.

i. Life's dreams, fulfilled or not, in order to still work on them.

j. New dreams, and old ones revived, so that higher energy and enthusiasm can yet allow new life to be born.

k. Ideas of death, dying and the hereafter to keep them positive.

l. Life's friendships/relationships, and their impact on us.

m. Use of leisure and its rewarding place in our daily life.

n. Hobbies and the enriching dimension they add to our life.

o. Retirement, to view it more than 'not working' in order to find the new life and love we have yet to give at this time of life.

p. Spirituality and prayer-life in order to give them priority in our daily life.

q. Later years and the life-style we'd like to pursue so that we make life happen, instead of just letting it just drag us along with little purpose.

r. Connection to our own inner spirit-power as the abundance of Christ's Spirit Power within us, so that our later years will not only be filled with awareness of our Higher Power, but will be bursting with all the life Christ's Spirit has yet to bring to fruition within us and our life.

3. <u>We start with a notebook to which sheets can be added</u>; we divide entries into decades of life (subdivide if necessary); start writing beginning with the present time, and then, go back and fill-in memories as things come to mind.

4. <u>In our autobiography-inventory, we:</u>

   a. Identify major life-stages, and see how they impacted us.

   b. Put the past in perspective by telling what we wisely learned.

   c. Find a pattern in life which gives a sense of direction for the present and future; the past is over, but the present and future can be changed.

d. Prepare for the next stage of the journey through whatever means possible.

e. Identify our life's impact on the world, and affirm where we made a great difference for the better because of our life, love and service to others.

5. <u>Our writing emphasizes experiences rather than just facts</u>. The meaning of events are seen from the perspective of our whole life, rather than isolated incidents. The importance of this writing lies not so much in telling life's story, but rather allows us to pull our life together. This writing creates a feeling of wholeness, integration, healing, and worth-whileness about our life.

II. A second major task to be accomplished in becoming a spiritual elder is to engage in intergenerational healing. Someone in the family-system started the wrong; someone else must absorb, face, forgive, and heal it so it will not be passed on to the future.

A. This healing is an important part of our personal inventory. In making an effort to heal intergenerational hurts, we, also, in the process, become healed by Christ. We're then enabled to pass on life, love, light and higher spiritual energy.

1. Making a commitment to Christ to be a healer in family, community, church, society, and the world is a role we may not neglect as we grow older. If spiritual-elder wisdom-keepers do not do this task, it will never be done.

B. In intergenerational healing, *we heal the dead* through our prayers and forgiveness for the living; *we heal the living* by our prayers and forgiveness for the dead.

1. All of us have been emotionally wounded as a child, even as a fetus. We don't have to dig around to find our wounds if we do not know from whence they came. We simply surrender these to the loving, forgiving presence of Christ. As we surrender them, healing happens and they're not passed-on.

C. Family patterns are not just personal, but are trans-generational. What one generation sows, another reaps, sometimes slowly, and sometimes skipping a generation or more. If unforgiveness is not resolved within the generation which created the conflict, it will be passed on to future generations until it's healed.

1. In growing up, we know that we inherit physical family traits; we inherit mental and spiritual ones as well. The good news is that *even one member* can be the instrument of peace in the healing of the family and family tree. Members with negative attitudes continue the non-love cycle. Members with Christ's love and higher spiritual energy pass on positive ones through the family.

2. As we grow older, we must take on the responsibility of being healers, healers within our own family-system primarily, as spiritual elders. Our prayer for intergenerational healing is essential to healthy eldering.

III. As we uncover what needs healing in ourselves and in our family system, we understand ourselves better and can choose to act differently from our previous script.

A. Our life-scripts are not cast in stone; they determine the course of our lives only when we let them. We can rewrite our story to bring about positive changes.

1. Our life-scripts, created in childhood, enabled us to thrive in our family, but now they no longer serve this function. We may not confuse this with who we really are, with who we are yet to become, and with how we are to live *now.*

a. Our individual script, rewritten as we become spiritual elders, is one of the most important factors which influence who we can yet become.

2. Just as we caught sin and weakness in our mother's womb, we can be healed from these, and not pass them on. We freely chose to give them to Christ, *even if we do not know what they are,* or *where they came from.*

3. Christ can heal the wounds we received even in the womb, (e.g.,emotional state of parents, loud, abusive words, hurtful actions, ancestral weakness, sin, etc.). Christ will heal all these hurts, if we simply give them to him.

a. Baptism healed the wound of original sin. Being healed of other sin, wrongs, and non-love requires spiritual growth, lived experience, our free choice, prayer, our personal request and openness to Christ's touch.

4. We simply bring the wound of our wrongs and hurts to Christ, rely on the Gifts of the Spirit given to us at Baptism and Confirmation as our tools, and believe that we will be healed, along with the woundedness and wrongs in our family tree. Sometimes we know these, sometimes not. The fact remains that when we daily give these to Christ, *he* knows what they are, and where they came from and *he* does the healing. The wrongs, then, are not passed on.

IV. When patterns of non-love in us, or our family-system, separate us from others, the reason is that we are out of communication with Christ in some meaningful way. Admission of this wrong sets the stage for reunion with him and for forgiveness.

A. An intimate, dynamic encounter with Christ brings healing and new life. He is not limited by time or space; past, present and future are the same to him. We choose to let him heal and transform us, and ask him to show us how to spread his life-giving love, life, light, positive energy, and presence all around us.

    1. Intergenerational love and non-love are great mysteries. Our task in becoming a spiritual elder is at least to begin the process of healing and wholeness. Someone else will take it from here and will pass on whatever we leave them.

B. The Father sent his Son for one reason only: that we might "have life and have it to the full." (John 10:10) Christ will never let us down; he wants to anoint us with his joy and high spiritual energy through his healing and forgiveness.

    1. Forgiveness is healing; healing is forgiveness. Forgiveness is the foundation for all healing. As we make this a primary task, future generations will be grateful, even if they will never know what we did until eternity.

    2. Each day, we send a healing blessing to our family, past, present and future. Healing and forgiveness *will happen*, through Christ, on God's time-schedule.

Some Questions to Ponder: Enabling Growth Through Transitions Unto Transformation

1. How do you feel about looking back so that you can reframe your life and get new meaning? What can you learn from wrongs you have done for which you are sorry?

2. Do you find it relatively more easy to admit your wrongs as you are getting older? Why or why not? What can you do to remedy this situation and become a healer?

3. Do you continue to blame your parents/family for your present behavior? How do you think you can rid yourself of this scapegoating during the second part of life so as to tap into higher, spiritual energy, and gain a new inner freedom?

4. How do you feel about writing your autobiography as a help to reframing your life during the next few years? Do you think it will be helpful to you? Why, or why not?

5. Has intergenerational healing been a part of your life up to this point? Are you aware of any wrongs which need to be healed so that they will not get passed on to the next generation? What can you do about this healing process to right the wrongs that you may have had nothing to do with? Those you may have had something to do with?

6. Admitting wrongs takes humility. As we get older, this is either easier or more difficult; how is it with you? How can you *choose* to release higher spiritual energy?

7. Do you view yourself as a spiritual elder in your family system who can take on this task of intergenerational healing? (It's one of the vital tasks of life before one dies.)

8. If you try this, and no one responds to your efforts, or if they are out of your life or deceased, do you still consider it worthwhile to try to be an instrument of healing? What are you planning to do about this?

9. Has the image of God, as Parent, and Trinity as Family, helped or hindered your spirituality? How can you let Christ change any negative connotations?

10. How do you feel about a daily blessing sent to your family-system for forgiveness and healing? What are other thoughts about this gesture? Is there another way?

List other questions you have about the eldering process. Use them for further reflections on your journey through transitions unto transformation as you grow into a spiritual-elder-sage.

Some Scripture Quotes:
To Affirm Growth in the Maturing Process

1. "Never act our of rivalry of conceit; rather, let all parties think humbly of others as superior to themselves, each of you looking to anothers' interest rather than to his own. Your attitude must be that of Christ..." (Phil 2:3-5)

2. "Learn to do good. Make justice your aim; redress the wronged...come now, let us set things right, says the Lord." (Is 1:17-18)

3. "The Lord said to Moses: 'Speak to the whole Israelite community and tell them: Be holy, for I, the Lord your God am holy.' " (Lv 19:2)

4. "My heavenly Father will treat you in exactly the same way unless each of you forgives his brother from his heart." (Mt 18:35)

5. "If anyone is in Christ, he is a new creation. The old order has passed away; now all is new! All this has been done by God who has reconciled us to himself through Christ and has given us the ministry of reconciliation." (2 Cor 5:17-18)

6. "Let us profess the truth in love and grow to the full maturity of Christ the head. Through him the whole body grows, and with the proper functioning of the members joined firmly together by each supporting ligament, builds itself up in love." (Eph 4:15-16)

7. "The dead man came out bound head and foot with linen strips, his face wrapped in a cloth. 'Unite him,' Jesus told them, 'and let him go free.' " (Jn 11:44)

8. "I am the true vine and my Father is the vine grower. He prunes away every barren branch, but the fruitful ones he trims clean to increase their yield...live on in me , as I do in you." (Jn 15:2,4)

9. "Let anyone who thinks he is standing upright watch out lest he fall!" (1 Cor 12)

Find some Scripture quotes which speak
to your heart at this time of life.

Step 11: Deepening Friendship With Christ

Sought through prayer and meditation to improve our conscious contact with God
as we understood him, praying only for knowledge of his will for us
and the power to carry that out.

*We seek to spend quality time deepening our friendship with Christ in new
ways, different from our earlier life, and according to our spiritual growth.
We stand open to the new mission he is calling us to do at this time of life.*

Promise 11: We will suddenly realize that God is doing for us what we could not
do for ourselves.

We'll spend quiet time with Christ and experience his creative power in us.

****

I. *Solitude* becomes a significant part of our prayer life as we grow older. It is the most simple form of prayer, yet the most profound. It is difficult to practice, unless we develop a personal friendship with Christ and realize that we are truly lovable.

> **A.** We all like to spend time with someone we love. If we love ourselves, we'll enjoy being alone with Christ. This kind of love-filled solitude is probably the most spiritually fruitful way we'll ever pray, whether or not we ever feel his presence.
>
> > **1.** Creating times of solitude is an essential task for becoming a spiritual elder. Slowing down in this way is vital to our becoming a vibrant, positive wisdom keeper who always has 'lots of love to give yet,' for his *will* for us is *to love.*
> >
> > **2.** How do we know if we are getting old we may ask. The answer is that *we get old when we stop loving.* When we stop loving, we stop living. As we enter into solitude with Christ, there's no such thing as getting old!
>
> **B.** We often think that we don't know how *to pray*, or we confuse *prayer* with *prayers*, instead of realizing that there are as many 'ways' as there are people.
>
> > **1.** *'Prayer'* is an attitude of heart, an inner solitude, a way to live: Christ present to me, and I to him. Actually, to *be a prayer* is the best prayer.
> >
> > **2.** *'To pray*,' (praying) means to go to a place apart, in quiet, where we can reflect on our friendship with Christ, and where we can listen to what he wants to tell us about the tasks he has lined up for us to yet do for him.

a. This is what Christ did each time he went to a place of solitude (to a desert, boat, wilderness, mountain, lake, to where no one else knew, out in his Father's Scripture of Creation), so that he could *pray* alone.

3. *'Prayers'* are simply thoughts, words, or actions which formalize what we reflect on during our solitude times with Christ. They are our way of helping us to stay focused, to express what we *want* or *need* to say to him, so that this precious friendship deepens and strengthens.

C. Our prayer-time and our prayerforms can be done alone or with others. They can take place in any activity that fills our day, provided we allow ourselves to be a conduit through which Christ's love, light, life, and Presence flow freely.

1. Prayer is simply living in mutual awareness of presence in love: Christ to me and I to him. This awareness is a combination of ***intention*** and ***attention***.

2. Our *intention* is to choose to be aware of his presence with us. Our *attention* keeps the flame alive in any way we can, and this makes us a *living prayer.*

3. In this process, we become aware that Christ loves us so much that literally he 'can't take his eyes off of us,' nor can we take ours off of him.

4. As we grow in this lived awareness, we are a living prayer. We become a spiritual-elder-sage through whom Christ's Presence is alive in the world.

5. Christ urged us to 'pray' always, not to 'say prayers' always. Once we realize this more intensely in our eldering process, we will never view our lives as useless because we can't work as we used to. As long as we love, we pray.

6. When we enter into this deeper prayer-life, our entire view of living a worthwhile life changes from lower, negative energy into higher, life-giving, positive, spiritual energy, and from *doing* to *being.* This empowers us with a renewed usefulness, and a new vocation evolves, one whose focus is love.

II. Another essential task during our eldering stage is to build this solitude into our daily schedule. We will thereby come to believe (especially as work life dwindles) that our primary vocation in our later years is truly a Ministry of Contemplation.

A. Contemplation is living in mutual awareness of Presence in love: he to me, I to him. Each moment holds a chance for a mutual exchange of affection between us.

B. This kind of prayer is a total response to life. It doesn't mean that we only talk; it also means we listen. We become quiet, and relish the love flowing between us.

    1. The goal of prayer is simply prayer, just as the saying of "I love you," is simply love. I articulate those realities as I express both my love and prayer. Love is just for loving and for nothing else and for no other reason. Prayer is the same; it is simply for encounter with Christ and for no other reason.

    2. The expression of love, through prayer forms, or to another person, comes from the felt reality of the experienced relationship with the beloved. The saying of love in "I love you" is the doing of the relationship of loving, for I put the beloved first always.

C. If we would do nothing in our prayer-life but to say "Yes," to the Christ-life that the Father wants to pour into us at the touch of the Spirit, all else would fall into place in our life's journey. Getting older would simply mean more loving 'yeses,' and our life would never grow stale, empty, or seem useless, _because of our love._

    1. From our 'yes' flows our 'Magnificat' (celebration) for all that the Father has done to us, at the touch of the Spirit. Each day brings us into a greater fullness of Christ, and into greater likeness of him. _This is our only reason for living._

        a. Neither Christ nor Mary knew _what_ they said 'yes' to; they only knew _who,_ and that was enough. Both knew that a Resurrection / Magnificat was coming but didn't know _when._ They trusted the Father and the Spirit; the Resurrection happened, and the Magnificat was sung in due time.

    2. With this realization, we know that our spirit can always stay young, that our attitude will always be youthful, and that our life will always be fruitful and very worthwhile. We'll never grow old if we always have love to give.

        a. We also know that _our_ Magnificat will be sung, and _our_ Resurrection with Christ will happen in the Father's good time, when the Spirit knows we're open and ready. _They_ will roll back the stone and put the music in our hearts.

III. As we grow older, we must take a fresh look at our _prayerforms._ We may no longer express love the same way we did in earlier days. Whether this is in loving others, or living in friendship with Christ, we need fresh expressions of love for both.

    A. Formal prayers need to be open to new ways. Just as we express a loving friendship in different ways as we mature in it, so also we must find fresh ways to enter into the solitude of our contemplative friendship with Christ.

1. If former, more structured prayerforms still feed our spirit and express our friendship with Christ at our new age, we keep them. If not, we must let them go, not as bad, but as having outgrown them. We need to switch from milk to more solid food and to give up the have-to in order to develop the want-to.

2. Maturing elders often feel guilty when they don't 'get their prayers in.' As we mature spiritually (the main goal of our older years), we learn that the guilt feeling comes from the fact that **we** have been in control of our prayer-life. Now, however, we need to let go and let Christ lead us to new heights and depths.

a. When we were not so mature or wise, we prayed in order that we would become holy. We now realize that this isn't correct; in our eldering years, we come to *believe* that *we are already holy, therefore, we pray.*

b. Christ has been with us all through life, taking the initiative, caring, inviting, calling, patiently waiting for us to grow into this realization. In our maturing years, we become aware of this tremendous gift that was with us all along: *the call to intimate friendship with him!*

c. This puts Christ in charge of our prayerlife. We need only to respond to his invitation, advances, and call to us to simply '*be with him,*' as he called the apostles to be. We just let him love us, and we love him back.

B. Have-to forms melt into more heart-expressed ones; we simply talk life over with him. Then, we discover new life by listening to what Christ is calling us to do for him at this time in life, different from our previous years.

1. We cannot solve the problems of later years with the tools of earlier ones in any other dimension of our lives. Neither can we stick to prayerforms and expressions of love which we have outgrown and which no longer serve us.

C. The *should* prayerforms yield more to *want-to* times of solitude wherein we are free to follow our hearts in ways that enrich this primary life-relationship. Christ will lead us into a friendship with him that we could never imagined.

1. We take time to go apart with him, so that he can speak to our heart. Just by being with him, we'll be better able to radiate him to the world. *Being* a prayer will be reflected in our *doing*, and the world will be a better place.

2. Prayer is for prayer, and for no other reason. The effect of the *pray-er* is the prayer. *Being* a prayer is our loving; *being* loving is our prayer. In this activity, the world will be different; we'll make a difference, and have fun doing it. We'll never grow old because we have much to give: our love!

IV. Some suggestions for developing solitude/contemplation may be helpful in our journey toward becoming a spiritual-elder-sage. Remember, who we are is how we pray.

    A. *Centering prayer*: is simple, yet profound. We:

        1. Find a quiet place; cut down on unnecessary noise.

        2. Set time limits; ten to thirty minutes is good.

        3. Relax; choose a posture which is easy to maintain.

        4. Close our eyes; this cuts down on distractions.

        5. Breathe deeply; inhale Christ's love and exhale it out to the world.

        6. Use a sacred word or short phrase; this keeps our thoughts focused.

        7. End the time slowly; use a short formal prayerform which is well-known.

    B. *Franciscan contemplation:* is mentally both active and quieting. We:

        1. Read a favorite Scripture passage.

        2. Use our imagination to put us into the passage.

        3. React to the passage through a creative act, music, art, writing, a poem, etc..

        4. Take a prayer-walk, listen to music and let Christ's Presence wash over us; slowly eat an orange, and marvel at its creation; go fishing, clean the fish and give them away; or, lie on the floor and offer ourselves to Christ as Francis did, naked.

Some Questions to Ponder :
Enabling Growth Through Transitions Unto
Transformation

1. What does 'prayer' mean to you, at *this age* of your life, as opposed to previous years? Is it changing? How? Are you at ease with any changes you have made or will make in your prayer-life, and in the prayerforms which express it?

2. What are your observations about the definitions of <u>prayer, to pray and prayers</u> as defined here? What are your definitions? What does Christ's 'pray always' mean?

3. How do you understand the deeper call to solitude during your older years? How does this resonate with your spirituality and prayerlife? What can you do about this?

4. How do you express the fact that you are a vibrant conduit through which Christ's love, light and life can flow to others each day? What is your symbol of this reality?

5. How and where do you spend quality solitude time by just *'being with Christ'?*

6. Have your prayerforms changed over the past few years? How? Did you feel that you were neglecting something by giving up some past forms in order to enter into a deeper kind of friendship with Christ as you mature? If they've not changed much, why not? Are they still helpful, or just being done from a sense of duty?

7. Where are your mountain tops? Your deserts? The places(s) into which Christ's Spirit can lead you so as to speak to your heart more deeply?

8. How does this solitude time with Christ help you to know what he wants you to do for him at this stage of life? How does this time strengthen you to move ahead?

9. Are you able to do the *'stand in front of the mirror'* prayerform, and believe it? How have you changed it to fit you and your needs? Do you find it helps or inhibits you?

10. How can the spirituality of the 'yes' and 'Magnificat' become a reality in your daily life, especially as you look toward your later years? How can you make these *yours?*

11. Where is Christ in your life now? Where do you want him during your later years?

List other questions you have about the eldering process. Use them for further reflections on your journey through transitions unto transformation as you grow into a spiritual-elder-sage.

Some Scripture Quotes:
To Affirm Growth in the Maturing Process

1. "Rejoice always, never cease praying, render constant thanks; such is God's will for you in Christ Jesus." (1 Thess 5:16-18)

2. "As for me and my household, we will serve the Lord." (Jos 24:15)

3. "Be firm and steadfast! Do not fear nor be dismayed, for the Lord, your God, is is with you wherever you go." (Jos 1:9)

4. "Whenever you pray, go to your room, close your door, and pray to your Father in private." (Mt 5:6)

5. "In your prayer, do not rattle on like the pagans. They think they will win a hearing by the sheer multiplication of words. Do not imitate them. Your Father knows what you need before you ask him. This is how you are to pray: Our Father in heaven, hallowed be your name, your kingdom come, your will be done on earth as it is in heaven. Give us today our daily bread, and forgive the wrong we have done as we forgive those who wrong us. Subject us not to the trial, but deliver us from the evil one." (Mt 6:7-13)

6. "It was not you who chose me, it was I who chose you to go forth and bear fruit. Your fruit must endure, so that all you ask the Father in my name he will give to you. The command I give you is this, that you love one another." (Jn 15:16-17)

7. "If two of you join your voices on earth to pray for anything whatever, it shall be granted to you by my Father in heaven. Where two or three are gathered in my name, there am I in their midst." (Mt 18:19-20)

8. "Let the word of Christ, rich as it is, dwell in you." (Col 3:16)

9. "Live on in me, as I do in you." (Jn 15:4)

10. "My entire being is ready to burst with the joy of the Lord, my spirit has stroked the radiant face of God. For God has looked upon me in my brokenness and weakness; yet, he has called me to be a brilliant light to his people. The Lord God has done incredibly wonderful things to me, and magnificent is his name."
(Lk 1:46-49)   (Adapted: Angelita)

Find some Scripture quotes which speak
to your heart at this time of life.

Step 12: Living and Sharing the Message of New Life and Love

Having had a spiritual awakening as the result of these steps, we tried
to carry this message to alcoholics, and to practice these principles
in all our affairs.

*We have had a spiritual awakening about becoming a spiritual-elder-sage.
We now resolve to carry this dynamic, positive energy to others through, with and in
Christ. We'll create more opportunities to witness this reality.*

Promise 12: All the promises of sobriety will always materialize if we work for them.

We'll live the good news of vital spiritual eldering and we'll share it.

****

I. Becoming a spiritual-elder-sage is not a finished piece of art. It is something we engage in every moment; it is a journey, not a place of anchoring, or a final port.

    A. When we choose *to accept* becoming a spiritual-elder-sage, we realize that this very choice is a culmination of all previous spiritual choices. This 'becoming' is an evolution to an inspired state of life in which our connection to the sacred energy within us is joined in a more fruitful way to our outward actions.

        1. We commit ourselves anew to cooperate with Christ's enabling, empowering grace, and to become the best spiritual-elder-sage possible. We renew our covenant with Christ and stand ready to share the life and love he's given us.

        2. We can now join the ranks of those who believe in debunking harmful myths about aging, and act according to our belief. The unique combination of age, experience, creativity, and wisdom can produce exciting inner growth, and an energy which has almost infinite potential, if we are open to possibilities.

        3. With revised vision, we look at:

            a. Our own spiritual growth over the years.

            b. Our desire to become a spiritual-elder-sage.

            c. How we accept our losses, and the gains from them on which we focus.

d. The skills and talents we have used, and the ones we still want to develop.

e. How we still want to use our greatest gift of all in our later years: *our love.*

4. We are now part of a generation which can view our next years with a vision that does not include an 'over the hill' attitude. The longevity factor in our country is greatly responsible for the fact that we can change. It allows (for the first time) a continuous study of getting older which emphasizes health and well-being instead of merely treating illness.

5. We go to our Source, Christ, to underscore our genuine human vitality, our unique creative power, and the radiant spiritual energy brought about by our age, experience, love, and wisdom which we have gathered over the years.

6. In our middle-and-beyond-years, we *can* develop extraordinary potential. These years can actually be our most creative and most satisfying. The years we have lived can become an asset leading to fuller, richer lives in our eldering process *if we reawaken our creativity and plan for a vital life.*

B. Centenarians are the fastest-growing age group in the US according to recent research on population in the country (PBS '04). As Church, we must rethink our role in this ministry in drastically new ways, both for our own maturing, and for the greater good of the people we serve. We can't keep things the same!

1. The results of our spiritual awakening must be carried to others, to both the younger and the older, or societal attitudes will never change, and we will have lost generations of creative wisdom, wit, experience and spirituality.

2. We are now in a position to see how our spirituality has impacted, and continues to impact, personally and intellectually, on all the spheres of our life.

3. With this lived wisdom, we are better able to see that spirituality is not about *beliefs*, but is rather about our contemplative capacities. We've come to an awareness that it is only through meditation and contemplative prayer that we can know our spiritual-elder-sage depth more completely at this time of life.

II. All church-communities must wake up to what's needed in the field of creative spiritual eldering. We cannot meet today's challenge by using tools of the past which mostly focused on, and treated, sickness, illness, disabilities, weaknesses and lacks.

A. It is still thought that people have all the spirituality they need once they reach adulthood. *This is profoundly not true.* We need to create totally new ways to enrich adult spirituality, and to refurbish workable older models, to meet new needs.

1. We need to stress a concept of dynamic spiritual growth and depth, along with wellness, creative energy, and a new kind of educational model which will enable and empower spiritual-elder-sages to further mature, and release lived wisdom.

2. Society and church must create new models for aging, and a fresh view which will see older people as the most valuable resource they have. The talents, skills, creativity, wisdom and spirituality of older adults are priceless.

3. We need to create ways to tap into this spiritual source of positive energy for the common good, and to challenge both church and society to maximize all the benefits of this tremendous, growing national and church resource.

B. Becoming a spiritual-elder-sage is different from just getting old. These are people who have done their homework, and are mentors and wisdom-keepers.

1. As spiritual-elder-sages, we first come into contact with our own spiritual depth; only then can we take this spirituality into whatever tasks we perform in the world. Our spirituality affects everything else in our lives.

2. As we work at becoming a spiritual-elder-sage, we can transform a downhill image of aging into an on-top-of-the hill higher energy one of new life. We realize that our later years can be a time of unimagined spiritual growth.

III. The relationship between *contemplation* and *action* is vital to our eldering spirituality. Without contemplation, we will not become a spiritual-elder-sage; but, without action, there will be no witness by the spiritual wisdom-keepers in church or society.

A. Becoming a spiritual-elder-sage does not center its reality in *religion*. It is bigger than that. Neither is our gleaned spiritual wisdom hung on to as if to be possessed. Our gifts must be given away so that others may benefit. From our spiritual eldering, love and life flow into the world, and the inter-play of these realities is essential to living our vocation as spiritual-elder-sages.

B. "How long the road is, but for all the time the journey has taken, how you have needed every second of it in order to learn what the road passes by."(Dag Hammerskjold, 1964, at 81)

1. The concepts of wisdom and maturity must be contrasted to those of hopelessness, downward sliding into uselessness, and senility, as people try to grapple with their perceptions of what it means to get older today.

2. In the recent past (1950'- 70's: Maslow; Allport), the focus was more on the psychosocial aspects of religion in a person's life, on their participation in institutional religions, and on disabilities, sickness, death and dying.

3. Since the '70's, literature (Fitzgibbons; Benson) is appearing which underscores a more holistic approach to the integration of spirituality and aging. It intertwines psychology and theology in life transitions. It also emphasizes on-going religious and spiritual development as having a central place in human lifespan development, alongside the moral and psychobiological.

IV. By sticking to the work of becoming a spiritual-elder-sage, we affirm energizing, creative attitudes coming to life within us. We are then ready to give them away!

A. As we walk tall as spiritual-elder-sages, we first deepen our prayer-life to be contemplative. Our contemplative prayer can range from centering prayer, through devotional prayerforms and reflections on sacred readings, to walking meditation, yoga, and t'ai chi. We simply create our own time and space for these.

B. As we become a spiritual-elder-sage, we prepare to mentor to others. <u>We:</u>

1. Pray for our mentee.

2. Listen, and give wisdom in small doses in response to questions.

3. Don't try to impress but lead out the budding wisdom that is already there.

4. Know that learning comes a little at a time.

5. Wait for teachable moments.

6. Develop a sense of humor.

7. Do not try to do everything.

8. Do not stand out.

9. Continue to grow.

10. Realize our own cycles of maturing.

11. Build a friendship with the mentee.

12. Then give them wings to fly!

C. As other life-giving gifts are given, we prepare to share them with others.

We:
    1. <u>Find wisdom</u> in, and appreciation for, wise sayings of elders.

    2. <u>Decide more creatively</u> about what's really important.

    3. <u>Get involved</u> in changing church and society's views/treatment of older adults.

    4. <u>Make time for fun things</u>, and see time as more precious than before.

    5. <u>Make plans to travel</u> where we've always wanted to go.

    6. <u>Think about, and plan</u> for our next decade, including hobbies to do.

    7. <u>Volunteer</u> where our skills and talents can best be used.

    8. <u>Plan</u> for our place of residence in our later years.

    9. <u>Prepare</u> our wake and funeral to be a true celebration of our life.

    10. <u>Try to be more realistic</u> with events, and better accept change and loss.

    11. <u>Recognize</u> and develop our skills and talents, and discover new ones.

    12. <u>Look for new careers</u>, or ways of sharing our wisdom and knowledge.

    13. <u>Cultivate</u> a greater appreciation of God's Scripture of Creation.

    14. <u>Try to become more creative</u>, even in lesser ways like rearranging a room.

    15. <u>Understand and appreciate</u> parents more.

    16. <u>Have increased interest</u> in our family tree, heritage, and legacy.

    17. <u>Find enjoyment</u> in lifelong learning.

    18. <u>Look for adventure</u>, and take reasonable risks to discover it.

    19. <u>Cope better</u>, become more mellow and forgiving, less explosive.

    20. <u>Don't really care</u> what others think, and don't depend on them for happiness.

21. <u>Become more joyful</u>, optimistic, grateful, tolerant, understanding and loving.

22. <u>Listen to our intuition</u>, and are more free to follow it.

23. <u>No longer get caught up in status</u>; we're free to go where we need to go.

24. <u>Focus on wellness</u>, and not on doctors curing us; we do more self-care.

25. <u>Learn</u> from ours and other's mistakes; we gain wisdom from this reflection.

26. <u>Laugh more</u>, and don't take things so seriously; we choose peace and quiet.

27. <u>Develop</u> our brain cells; some die, but the remaining ones can get smarter!

28. <u>View wisdom</u> as a central virtue of life; we become wiser in our eldering.

29. <u>Become more assertive</u> and less aggressive; our self-discipline increases.

30. <u>Revel in our uniqueness</u>, our love, beauty and goodness is non-repeatable.

31. <u>Open ourselves</u> to give love and hugs, and to *being* loved and hugged.

32. <u>See beauty and love everywhere</u>, and all ground as sacred and precious.

33. <u>Help others deepen their friendship with Christ,</u> on their spiritual journey.

34. *<u>Accept</u> what we cannot change, change what we can, and **now** have the lived wisdom as a spiritual-elder-sage to know the difference!*

Some Questions to Ponder:
Enabling Growth Through Transitions
Unto Transformation

1. How do you know when you or someone else is old? What is your attitude now?

2. How are you becoming a spiritual-elder-sage in specific ways? How does this affect those around you?

3. What major turning points have you had these past few years which have affected your attitude and growth in the eldering process--for better, or for worse? How can you sift out what was beneficial, and pass what you learned on to others, in order to help them develop into spiritual-elder-sages?

4. Have you done any reading recently about this transition stage of life? How can you share what you have leaned with others who are still in the dark about eldering?

5. How do you envision yourself as a spiritual-elder-sage?

6. What do you hope for as you get older, wiser, and more contemplative? How can your dreams and visions impact on your spiritual community, and on society?

7. What are your *best* things about eldering, the *easiest*, and the *worst?* How can you help others in their eldering process by sharing what you've learned about your own?

8. What skills and talents can you develop to make the world better at this time in your life? Where can you find life-giving, love-giving involvement? What other gifts have been given to you which can be added to your talent-list of previous years?

9. What values have you learned from eldering? Which ones have helped you to balance losses with gains? How can you help others with your learned wisdom?

10. How are you trying to become a contemplative spiritual-elder-sage, in this time of life? How are you planning for growth, with Christ, in this vital eldering task?

List other questions you have about the eldering process. Use them for further reflections on your journey through transitions unto transformation as you grow into a spiritual-elder-sage.

Some Scripture Quotes:
To Affirm Growth in the Maturing Process

1. "Go, therefore, and make disciples of all nations ... and know, that I am with you always, until the end of the world." (Mt 28:19,20)

2. "Go into the whole world and proclaim the good news to all creation." (Mk 16:15)

3. "But Moses said to God: 'Who am I that I should go to the Pharaoh...'? He answered, 'I will be with you;...Is it not I, the Lord? Go, then! It is I who will assist you in speaking and will teach you what you are to say.' " (Ex 4:11-12)

4. "There is an appointed time for everything...a time to be born, and a time to die; a time to plant, and a time to uproot the plant." (Eccl 3:1-2)

5. "To the elders among you, I, a fellow elder, a witness of Christ's sufferings and a sharer in the glory that is to be revealed, make this appeal. God's flock is in your midst; give it a shepherd's care. Watch over it willingly as God would have you do, not under constraint...but generously." (1 Pt 5:1-2)

6. "It is no longer I who live, but Christ who lives in me." (Gal 2:20)

7. "I will do no boasting about myself unless it be about my weakness... in order that I might not become conceited I was given a thorn in the flesh...three times I begged the Lord that it might leave me. He said to me, 'My grace is enough for you, for in weakness power reaches perfection.' And so, I willingly boast of my weakness instead, that the power of Christ may rest upon me." (2 Cor 12:5,7-9)

8. "You are a people sacred to the Lord, your God; he has chosen you from all the nations on the face of the earth to be a people peculiarly his own." (Dt 7:6)

9. "The Lord came and revealed his presence, calling out as before, 'Samuel, Samuel!' Samuel answered, 'Speak, Lord, for your servant is listening.' " (1 Sm 3:10)

Find some Scripture quotes which speak
to your heart at this time of life.

Bibliography -- Helpful Readings

1. Bianchi, E. *Aging as a Spiritual Journey.* New York: Crossroads. 1984

2. Bianchi, E. *Elder Wisdom: Crafting Your Own Elderhood.* New York: Crossroads. 1994

3. Bortz, William M. *Dare to be 100.* New York: Fireside, Simon & Schuster. 1996

4. Dychtwald, Ken. *Age and Power: How the 21st Century Will be Ruled by the Old.* New York: Jeremy P. Thatcher/Putnam, a Member of Penguin Putnam, Inc. 1999

5. Fischer, Kathleen. *Winter Grace: Spirituality and Aging.* Nashville, TN: Upper Room Books. 1998

6. Johnson, Richard P. *Body, Mind, Spirit.* Ligouri, MO: Ligouri Publications. (Dr. Johnson has many other fine resources.)

7. Kimble, Melvin E. et al. (Editors). *Aging, Spirituality and Religion: A Handbook.* Minneapolis: Fortress Press. 1995
(There is now a Volume 2; published in 2003 from the same publisher.)

8. Moberg, Daniel O. *Aging and Spirituality: Spiritual Dimensions of Aging Theory, Research, Practice and Policy.* New York: Haworth Pastoral Press. 2001

9. Roszak, Theodore. *America the Wise: The Longevity Revolution and the True Wealth of Nations.* Boston/New York: Houghton Mifflin Company. 1998

10. Roszak, Theodore. *Longevity Revolution: As Boomers Become Elders.* Berkeley Hills, CA: Berkeley Books. 2001 (revision of #9.)

NOTE: This is a fairly new field of enrichment which is just now beginning to reach non-academic status. You will find other topics dealing with 'eldering' (though not under that title) in the public library in the following number categories: 155's; 158's; 159's; 208's; 248's; 291's; 305's; 612's; and the 613's. In each, there are subcategories.

Some topics deal with nutrition, some with exercise, health, wellness and spirituality. It will be a great learning experience just to browse the books and find what appeals to you at this time of life. Just search the stacks to find a topic or title which 'jumps out at you.' The effort alone offers an opportunity for personal growth, plus: it's <u>free!</u> Other good resources are the Internet and your local bookstores.

Good luck in becoming a Wise Spiritual-Elder-Sage. God's blessings on you.

Use this space to jot down titles and sources
which appeal to you.

<u>Prayer for Serenity</u>

God, grant me the serenity
to accept the things I cannot change,
the courage to change the things I can,
and the wisdom to know the difference --
living one day at a time,
enjoying one moment at a time,
accepting hardship as a pathway to peace;
taking, as Jesus did,
this sinful world as it is,
not as I would have it;
trusting that you will make all things right
if I surrender to your will --
so that I may be reasonably happy
in this life,
and supremely happy with you
forever in the next.

Amen.

"Act justly, Love Tenderly.
Walk humbly with your God." -- Micah 6:8